"Profit and purpose are often seen as being mutually exclusive. In her thoroughly enjoyable new book, Joanne Sonenshine demonstrates by insight and example why this is far from the truth, and how business can find new sources of value while simultaneously serving society."

GIB BULLOCH, Author, *The Intrapreneur: Confessions of a Corporate Insurgent*

"In today's polarized, negative environment, distrust of big business may be one of the only unifying forces. Yet Sonenshine provides a much needed, and inspiring perspective on how business can be a force for good. She demonstrates with powerful stories how companies credibly pursue profitability in ways that are both ethical and intentional in creating a better society."

LAURA GITMAN, Chief Operating Officer, Business for Social Responsibility (BSR)

"Through her own unique journeys and partnerships, Sonenshine illustrates how corporate values actually lead to corporate profits, illuminating why businesses—and the leaders within them—must continue to be held accountable for the future of our workers, our communities, and our planet."

JOE GIZZI, Media Group Strategy Director

"As a company co-founder of products made by freed women, I am grateful that companies and conscious consumers are using purchasing power to address critical social issues like slavery, poverty, and trafficking. *Purposeful Profits* shares examples of this new way forward, and how business decisions impact the other end of a supply chain. Every purchase matters, and Sonenshine offers a close up look at how businesses are meeting the challenge of leading with their power for good."

KATHERINE JEFFERY, Ph.D., Co-Founder, CAUSEGEAR

"In *Purposeful Profits*, Joanne highlights the growing trend among business leaders to value a company's mission as highly as its profit. As a business leader and social entrepreneur, making a difference for the communities where we work is paramount. There is no mutual exclusivity between doing the right thing for your stakeholders and doing the right thing for your business. This book is a must read for any business leader and also will help all readers recognize that times are changing for the improvement of our planet."

JEHIEL OLIVER, Chief Executive Officer, Hello Tractor

"By weaving together personal stories, observations from traveling the world, and conversations with corporate leaders, in *Purposeful Profits* Joanne Sonenshine illustrates the importance of corporations stepping up as leaders for social change. But rather than focus exclusively on the corporate perspective, like many of the academic tomes do, Sonenshine highlights the workers who make it happen and without whom the businesses couldn't succeed. It's their empathy, resourcefulness, and dedication that propels companies forward. *Purposeful Profits* delivers useful and inspiring insights for anyone investigating or working in Corporate Social Responsibility."

JAMES ROONEY, Executive Director, DICK's Sporting Goods Foundation

"Sonenshine shares the human stories behind those who are working to change businesses from within, and challenges us all to ask ourselves if we are doing all we can to achieve the much needed transformation of business."

YASMINA ZAIDMAN, Chief Partnerships Officer, Acumen

Also by Joanne Sonenshine

ChangeSeekers:
Finding Your Path to Impact

PURPOSEFUL PROFITS

INSIDE SUCCESSFUL BUSINESSES
MAKING A POSITIVE GLOBAL IMPACT

Joanne Sonenshine

CONNECTIVE IMPACT

Published in Arlington, Virginia by Connective Impact LLC.

Print ISBN: 978-0-9994152-2-1
eBook ISBN: 978-0-9994152-9-0
Library of Congress Control Number: 2018912608

For Mom and Dad.

You have always taught me the values of kindness, curiosity, hard work, and keeping an open mind.

I am forever proud to be your daughter.

For Each of You, We Are Proud to Share a Portion of Proceeds with GlobalGiving.

GlobalGiving

*Transforming Aid and Philanthropy
to Accelerate Community-Led Change.*

www.globalgiving.org

Table of Contents

Introduction

The factories dotted the skyline, and their dark, deep plumes of smoke mixed with the dusty fields upon which they sat, creating a cloudy sadness all around them. I remember assembly lines of people pouring in and out of the buildings at opening and closing. Shoulders hunched and faces worn, laborers were the heartbeat of Cleveland, Ohio for decades. Soon, the layoffs came from the behemoths merging and instigating buyouts. BP, KeyBank, LTV Steel, and Ford Motor Company were just a few of the big named companies wheeling and dealing.

As a child, Corporate America to me meant high-rises filled with the money-hungry, taking over the city of industrial workers where I grew up. Government officials and the local news further branded their names into my subconscious, as the troubled economy of my hometown rested at their doors. Big business in Cleveland in the 1980s translated into fewer local jobs, a sagging economy and dirty rivers and streams that prohibited my friends and me from dipping even our big toes into Lake Erie.

In the decades since, a lot has changed. Companies are different. Laborers are different. Business aims are different. Despite continued challenges, Cleveland's communities are no longer captives to a dirty Corporate America as they were in the 1980s. Technology, medicine, and energy have taken over. The evolution has been a good one for cities like Cleveland. This evolution has been a good one for all of us. Sometimes, though, that realization is overwhelmed by memories of what happened in the past.

For decades, companies were seen as conglomerates simply out to make money and provide products for consumption, just like those in Cleveland in the 1980s. While some of the aims of business have not changed, and making money is still very important, the role of business leaders within companies is evolving fast. Empathy, emotional connections to stakeholders across the globe, and an interest in improving our planet, have shifted the mission of some of the biggest companies into impact-makers for social and environmental change. The journey of businesses from being purely money hungry to acting as societal game changers has been told in many forms, and by many people. It's important to hear about what it takes to change the game, though, from those calling the shots, and making the change happen. How has that evolution taken shape, and what does that mean for the future of global companies? How can companies build on this progress and make significant change in the world, while still being profitable and successful? How has the definition of success changed for companies? How have they imbedded the humanistic view that comes with seeing how the rest of the world lives? Has business found a new image for itself? Which elements of the new paradigm of business take into account the notion of our greater purpose and doing the right thing?

These are some of the questions this book aims to answer.

Companies are made up of people with hearts, dynamic minds, and general interests in doing "good." It's easy to forget that there are emotions and feelings that lie behind the brands we chastise or question. I have met some amazingly inspiring people working for some of the most criticized companies. They have reminded me there is a force for good that lies behind the neon signs and food counters. It cannot be ignored that as the world becomes more interconnected, and companies rely upon populations from the most remote parts of the world to produce their products, that empathy and humanism will ensure companies become our most promising leaders for societal change.

To get a sense of this paradigm shift, I harken again back to Cleveland. In 1986, British Petroleum (BP) bought the majority share of Standard Oil of Ohio ("Sohio") and the corporate takeover of one of the most iconic images from my youth (the Sohio gas station) was underway. BP had built the second tallest building in Cleveland (now third), and I can still remember the excitement around me from having a foreign corporate conglomerate take ownership of my city. Why Cleveland was chosen as one of the biggest (perhaps the biggest?) takeovers for BP in North America was due largely to the city's history as a center for oil refinery in the late 1800s, and the abundance of steel and manufacturing centered in the city. There may have been other reasons—cheaper labor? The promise of a quality education for families? A reasonable cost of living? Whatever the reasons, BP's brand was in Cleveland to stay, and those of us who grew up there remember it well. Most of those memories, though, were about managing the tough emotions of a city adjusting to big business. This included layoffs, wealth gaps, difficult politics, and demographic shifts.

Cleveland was by no means alone in managing this struggle. Hostile takeovers were common in the 1980s, and Gen Xers like me lived through many. In the decades since, however, we learned that success need not be at the cost of people or planet.

The initial push for businesses to operate for profit, at the cost of local jobs or perception, began during the Industrial Revolution, when the world fought intellectual battles around capitalism into the early part of the nineteenth century. With information flows increasing, and news about business wins and losses literally littering local streets after Samuel Morse invented the telegraph, shareholders began to call the shots. Corporations had to make money for their investors, or they were out of business overnight.[1] Business became a tool for the people, to buy and sell at their whim, and wealth became the priority.

The need to showcase wealth became even more critical during the early part of the 20th century, when the world was at war, depression was mounting, and the distinction

---

1. http://www.laits.utexas.edu/~anorman/long.extra/Projects.F97/
    Stock_Tech/page1.htm

between the haves and have-nots grew exponentially. Relying on corporate wealth to further drive motivations in supporting big business was risky during this time, but for those who took the risk, the payoff was big.

In more modern history, the gap between rich and poor has been a topic of political and social debates, and big business has consistently played a role in widening or shortening that gap, in large part because of those individuals who contribute money through share purchases, board direction, or by holding debt for companies' use in growth and innovation. For those who weren't stakeholders in this ever-changing dynamic of stock market shifts or company invest- ment strategies, a view of big business as the enemy of the little guy stuck.

Yet, at the end of the day, companies exist to provide customers (us) services and products. If not for busi- nesses, there would be no food on our tables, clothes on our backs, furniture in our homes, or gas in our cars. Even with a significant transformation, away from manufacturing and into technology and innovation, the list of necessities supplied to us by businesses, is endless. We can't function without them, many are employed by them, and we clearly need to live in harmony with them.

Forbes recently published an article about the emerging way of doing business.[2] The article shares data from two studies in which 40 percent of respondents indicated, "The goal of business should be to 'improve society' (second only to 'generate jobs' in terms of priorities)." The article goes on to state: "Today's workforce is rejecting the old Milton Friedman notion that the only social responsibility of business is to maximize profits; they think business should also be trying to make a positive difference in the world." In a recent social media post, as an example, an employee of household products company, SC Johnson, shared that she loved being able to connect her work to a higher purpose. She added a quote from SC Johnson President, Fisk Johnson: "We measure our success not by the financial report of the next quarter, but by what we can do to make the world better for this generation and the next."

Without burying the headline, here's the kicker: Despite remnant negative views of business as profit hungry or its leaders only out for themselves, **businesses ARE making a positive difference in the world**. And a big one at that.

---

2. https://www.forbes.com/sites/michelegiddens/2018/08/03/rise-of-b-corps-highlights-the-emergence-of-a-new-way-of-do-ing-business/?utm_campaign=coschedule&utm_source=twit-ter&utm_medium=BCorporation#6ee138cb2ed2

There have been countless articles written, and even more recently, books published, about the evolving role of business as a positive force in society. I have no intention of using this book to rehash these stories, or repeat all of the statistics that point to business as our best hope for true social and environmental impact, though I wholeheartedly agree that this is true. Instead, I look forward to showcasing *why* businesses have become so closely tied to social impact and environmental responsibility and focus on a unique set of stakeholders often ignored when talking about socially conscious businesses.

For many of the most progressive companies making change in the space of sustainability and social impact, the root cause for these investments stems not just from consumer interest or demand in seeing them do the right thing (though that plays a big role, which can't be denied and again, is not the topic of this book), but instead as a show of support for those working in some of the most impoverished nations, without whom our clothes would not be made, food not grown, and shoes not fit for our feet.

Much has been made about the need to understand and recognize the role of stakeholders (i.e., employees, factory workers, managers, farmers, community leaders, and so on) within socially and environmentally responsible businesses. But still, very few of their stories have been told. Some of these individuals have risked their lives, their families, and their communities to help make business a force for good, but rarely, if ever, do we read their stories in the headlines, or see them profiled in corporate annual reports (though that is also changing).

They are the unseen laborers. They are parents working thousands of miles away from their families in order to make a living to support their children's education. They are children working in the city centers, rather than attending school, so their parents can raise their siblings instead of work in the local factory. They are women toiling in fields in obscene temperatures, picking rice that gets packaged in orange boxes and delivered to our grocery stores. They are the nameless faces that continually go unrecognized. They are the social entrepreneurs, finding ways to combine mission and profit. Or they are managers advocating for those who cannot advocate for themselves. This book not only tells some of their stories, but also demonstrates by the stories included within, the evolution of businesses that are making the effort and commitment to serve these individuals better, to recognize their essential contribution, and see the opportunity to add to the greater good.

While traveling with some of the most high-profile corporate leaders, I have been overwhelmed with emotion as these individuals finally take stock of who is actually doing the work for their organizations. The second these leaders finally "get it" is the second I know hope is at hand. When business leaders are able to see with their own eyes who provides the products that makes the millions of dollars for the company, I see their empathy burst at the seams, metaphorically crashing the four walls of their office buildings. Like me, they see there are stories to be told, credit to be shared.

This realization happens all the way down to farm gate or factory door, when leaders recognize that decisions have very real impacts, in faraway places, that can't be ignored. Of course, there has been a journey for big business to reach this place of empathy, and continuing to tell these stories of those that would normally go untold, hopefully will help accelerate a change in business and the thinking of business leaders even more.

As our planet becomes more closely tied via the Internet, virtual reality, social media, and live video, businesses can no longer ignore what is happening within their supply chains, brands, and employee bases. Not only can they not ignore it, they have an opportunity to shout from the rooftops about some of the amazing stories, and showcase that *these* are faces of their successful companies. They can lead by exemplifying that the acquisition of money will no longer be the company's only concern. This recognition will shift the paradigm of how businesses are run, including how decisions are made and profits as well. With this evolution comes an entirely new approach to business.

While there are endless stories to tell, and it would be impossible to share them all, this book attempts to take you behind the scenes, to understand the complexities of decision-making, and the push-pull that exists between profits and impact. We have come a long way since the 1980s, when soot filled the skies of the Cleveland, Ohio of my youth. The simple truth is that it should not be difficult to make choices for a company about doing the right thing, giving back to communities, or working to change the planet. This book will shed light on what does go into those decisions, and who is often involved. My hope is that you will take with you some inspiration, a greater appreciation of what it takes to do the right thing as a business leader, and recognition that the world is full of some pretty amazing people changing the shape of business and social impact all at once.

CHAPTER ONE

Authenticity and Education: Community and Brand Values

Anyone my age (I'm 41) remembers the late 1980s movie, *Working Girl*, starring Melanie Griffith. The movie is about a young woman, Griffith, working to get herself noticed at a large corporation, Petty Marsh. Griffith's role as a witty and smart, yet untested secretary, contrasts with that of her boss, played by actress Sigourney Weaver, who will stop at nothing to take credit for Griffith's creative ideas. Without giving away too much, the moral of the story is that neither greed nor corruption will ever win, but for those wanting to operate in a more righteous space, they can be assured of a tough road ahead. Coupled with that lesson is some serious attention placed on the success of Petty Marsh, and the winner-takes-all mentality that made the 1980s an era all about big shoulder pads, big hair, and a heck of a lot of corporate greed.

According to a 2002 article in *The Economist*, greed can be good for the economy if properly governed. This notion that greed was the right approach for business captured the 1980s perfectly.[3] At the time, success was purely measured by companies swallowing up other companies and investment bankers buying and selling corporate holdings to make the most money possible. The flip side, which was hidden behind the money, glitz, glamour, and appeal of 1980s business, were workers laid off in massive takeovers. But when you Google "1980s business," the images are full of private jets, champagne, and bankers. Greed, for business, was good.

Like anything in the extreme, though, something had to give. The savings and loan crisis of the late 1980s and early 1990s began a ripple effect of bank closures and instituted a more critical view on financial markets as a means for personal (and corporate) wealth. The role of corporations as pure money machines, once lauded and admired, began to shift ever so slightly as both the public and business leaders wondered if this past level of greed was actually good for business.

---

3. https://www.economist.com/special-report/2002/05/16/is-greed-good

Along with the way companies prioritized money making in the 1980s, there was evidence of corporations taking advantage of those most critical to their success—their consumers. One analogy to describe the relationship between corporate America and the consumers of the 1980s is that of a wall, big and concrete. The wall separated company stakeholders from the realities of the production processes used for operations. Customers just didn't have a sense of what went on behind closed doors, and companies liked it that way. Each had a role: consumers bought things, and companies made money.

As an example of the non-symbiotic relationship between customers and companies, 3M, the company now most known for its sticky notes and wall hooks, was outed in a recent exposé published by *The Intercept* and reproduced for *Fast Company*[4] around a product that grew in popularity over the '80s. In the report, 3M—as well as the U.S. Environmental Protection Agency—reportedly knew that the chemicals they formulated in the 1970s for non-stick cooking pans (known to most of us as Teflon) were extremely dangerous, not only to the environment, but also to

---

4. https://www.fastcompany.com/90212342/3m-knew-your-non-stick-pan-was-poisoning-you-in-the-70s

human health. Over the years, rumors have swirled as scientists issued more research about the safety (or lack thereof) of non-stick pans used in cooking. Still, there was never any attempt by 3M to either repudiate or confirm any of the data that existed.

According to *The Intercept*, the company, instead, embarked on a massive cover-up effort starting as early as 1975, working for nearly four decades to protect its customers from knowing the truth: that Teflon is indeed toxic and extremely harmful to humans and as a release into the atmosphere. 3M was a power house company in the 1980s (and still is) and did little to concern itself with keeping its customers from buying its nonstick pans.

Today, 3M has turned things around and boasts a corporate strategy around sustainability and "Improving Lives,"[5] journeying a long way from the days of lies, deceit, and toxic decision-making (or let's hope!).

There are many similar stories of companies thriving among lies or covering up truth to ingratiate consumers and other stakeholders. This was easy to do in the 1980s, when there was more limited commu-

---

5. https://www.3m.com/3M/en_US/sustainability-us/

nication, technology, and oversight. It's no surprise that consumers were pessimistic of corporate intention for years, and many continue to be despite the progress toward purpose and impact we see today.

Where did the shift toward greater positive action begin? Like the Berlin Wall that came crumbling down in 1989, allowing a generation to embrace democracy and establish more healthy relationships with government, similarly, the corporate mantra of greed and disobedience so prevalent in the 1980s began seeping through the concrete walls, allowing the public on the other side to learn the truth.

For starters, secrets were no longer withheld. As the financial markets shifted toward more transparency, so, too, did corporations. Financial statements and operating information became more available to shareholders, customers, and employees, and companies became more accountable for their actions. Additionally, the acceleration of technology allowed for more definitive science to back arguments against companies like 3M.

From inside the walls, corporate executives had to decide whether they would continue operating as before, with secrecy and shortcuts, or whether they would lead with conviction and integrity, and run the risk that transparency could shine the light on practices or operations that weren't up to par. Action from within was still rare back in the 1980s, though less so as the decade moved on. There is one company, however, whose founder instituted a culture of social giving and community engagement that has grown and evolved along with its customers, prioritizing doing the right thing and being morally righteous. The Hershey Company is lauded for its mission-driven work regularly and sets an example for other companies working on perfecting the balance between transparency and customer loyalty.

Milton Hershey, the father of Hershey's chocolate, was born in 1857 on a farm in Central Pennsylvania. Despite a lack of encouragement to pursue education by his parents, as well as failed attempts at starting various businesses, Hershey created one of the most iconic brands in all of U.S. history.

Journeying through difficulties making a living, Hershey, a relentless entrepreneur, solidified his future by breaking ground on his first factory in 1905 in Lancaster, Pennsylvania. His company grew in profitability and stature and became successful quickly.

Hershey and his wife, Catherine, found themselves unable to have children. With fortunes amassing, the Hersheys founded the Milton Hershey Industrial School in 1909 to pass on their legacy to the next generation. The school was a haven for orphans and ensured all students had proper clothes, food, and health.[6]

The Milton Hershey School is still a place of educational excellence for children facing extreme economic or social hardship. While visiting the company in 2017, I heard two Milton Hershey high school students speak about their personal experiences, traumas, and hopes and dreams. I will never forget their maturity, passion, and intelligence, and admire their dedication to education and career advancement, despite the challenges they've faced throughout their young lives.

Milton Hershey placed great emphasis on philanthropy, one of the values he gained from his upbringing, and and the focus on purpose has stayed with the company since its inception. This dedication resonates with all employees of The Hershey Company. Their intent on making good chocolate, and giving back to communities around them, is clear by the partnerships and projects they are part of, as an example.

When thinking about the need to prioritize purpose and values in a company like Hershey, the sheer size and scope of its remit can seem overwhelming to those responsible for its profits. The pressure to do "good" while making money for the company does not

---

6. https://www.mhskids.org/about/school-history/milton-s-hershey/

intimidate the Hershey employees I've met, however. In fact, many believe that doing "good" and making money go hand in hand.

Tawiah Agyarko-Kwarteng has worked with different types of organizations trying to change the world. Working for Hershey provides her one of the most formidable ways to change the future within her country of birth— Ghana.

Tawiah was born in Kumasi, Ghana, the youngest of four children. Tawiah grew up on a university campus where her mother taught as a professor. Her father was a hydrogeologist, initially supporting government projects but later working for nonprofit World Vision, drilling boreholes in rural communities lacking access to water.

When Tawiah was four, she moved to Oxford in the United Kingdom, where her mother attended graduate school. Education was the highest priority for Tawiah's family, and when Tawiah returned to Ghana at age eight, she attended the top schools in the country, including one of the region's best boarding schools.

Originally Tawiah wanted to be an architect. When her father began taking her and her siblings on trips to various World Vision project sites, however, Tawiah and her brothers and sisters encountered very different ways of life than they were used to. Her parents always explained that their family was fortunate, well educated, and in some ways unique compared to other families in Ghana. But it wasn't until Tawiah was about 16 years old that she realized the hardships of those living in more remote locations, where water, shelter, and education were hard to come by. These experiences made a huge difference in how Tawiah saw the world—and changed her path forever.

In University Tawiah opted to study development like her father, with the ultimate intention of changing lives and improving the world. After her studies she performed one year of mandatory voluntary service as a research assistant working on short- and medium-term development plans related to local government systems. She was accepted into Harvard University in 2002 where she received a Master's Degree in Public Administration in International Development.

After spending nearly nine years working for nonprofit World Education in both Boston and Ghana, Tawiah was hired by Hershey to help the company understand the local community context in Ghana and the rest of West Africa, where Hershey sources its cocoa. Additionally, Tawiah helps ensure the effective roll out of all of Hershey's sustainability and community development activities and that farmers and their families are at the center of programs.

Tawiah admitted that over the years, companies have struggled to adequately understand the local contexts of rural regions where efforts to support their corporate successes are underway. Large companies may not have the presence in certain regions where, ultimately, they should have a better sense of what motivates individuals to perform and/or contribute to a broader mission. One of the things that has prohibited the direct engagement with stakeholders in rural communities (both those that are producers and even those that are consumers) is a lack of understanding about the opportunity for rural development to positively impact a company's bottom line.

When thinking about her move from World Education to working with Hershey, Tawiah admitted that she had been questioning the effectiveness of nonprofits for long-term sustainability. She saw too many community members become dependent on "handouts." She believed that as Hershey focused on farmers, there was a more viable option for longer-term economic development, as Hershey's practice is to work with farmers through long-term buying contracts and business relationship building. To Tawiah, this is a win-win for Hershey and for other companies engaged in social good. They develop longer term, more effective relationships with stakeholders (producers and consumers) and take advantage of more sustainable business practices for greater efficiency—and ultimately profitability.

Photo courtesy of Tawiah Agyarko-Kwarteng

At their core, companies are still companies and are commercially driven. Tawiah recognizes that will not change. But leading with a social mission benefits communities in ways that would never happen otherwise.

The role of business as a driver for social good can be improved upon and scaled according to Tawiah. For example, companies are learning to tap into additional sources of funding to test new routes of innovation and creativity, especially if leadership is unwilling to move away from pure commercial priorities.

Collaborating with the Bill and Melinda Gates Foundation, in partnership with The World Cocoa Foundation, for example, has helped Hershey's focus on new and emerging issues like women's empowerment and income diversification for farming households. These engagements also open the minds of company leaders who may have been uber-focused on only selling product. Leveraging partnerships for innovation also build out new investment pathways for companies willing to take that next step.

While big business is still about making money, and that will never change, its leaders understand more and more that they have a key role to play in transforming the world as we know it. Hershey is an example of a company recognizing its role, all the while ensuring equity and equality in the process.

But for Tawiah, there is more work to do. Governments still question the role of business as a societal mover, so educating local stakeholders about companies as progressive partners is ongoing. Companies can continue learning from local contexts, too, and listening to their partners to learn about the specific needs of their communities must be a priority. Companies need to adapt to the changes and needs of their stakeholders to be effective, which is a role Tawiah is honored to play for Hershey. Tawiah takes her personal sense of purpose very seriously and is driven by integrity and a passion to improve the world around her. She is driven to impact those who have gone without, like those she saw when working with her dad in rural southern Ghana. Her memories of towns with no running water, people with no access to education, and the faces of children with no future never leave her.

Tawiah still holds education up to its highest regard, working for a company that does the same, and investing in the future of Ghana through a family foundation she, her siblings and mother started in honor of her late father. She feels right working for a purpose-driven company, even one that makes a big profit. She is confident in the knowledge that Hershey is always exploring new and innovative ways to make their footprint one that's positive and impactful.

LESSONS LEARNED: Being truthful about misgivings, shortcomings, or opportunities to improve is always preferred over lack of transparency. Dedicated leadership and employees, particularly those who believe in the corporate mission, can help a company stay on track with its social impact. Contrary to what we believed in the '80s, greed is never good. Understanding global contexts will help businesses make informed and proper decisions for long-term sustainability in regions where customers, employees, suppliers, and other stakeholders are most meaningful.

CHAPTER TWO

Balance of Power: Righteous Leadership and Preservation

Between 1986 and 1990, at least eight major policies were instituted within the United States that kicked off a trend away from the "dirty" behavior implicit in the early 1980s, and toward a more responsible relationship between large corporations and their stakeholders.

For example, in 1986, the United States passed the Superfund Amendments and Reauthorization Act (SARA), reauthorizing elements of the Superfund Act, which aimed to enforce the illegal practice of dumping hazardous waste and increased the focus on human health as it related to industrial waste.

In 1987, the government passed the Water Quality Act, overhauling how industries and communities managed water pollution. Environmental and social legislation then saw 1989 as a revolutionary year, with the U.S. ratifying its position in the Montreal Protocol on ozone-depleting chemicals. This was also the year of the infamous Exxon Valdez oil spill, when an Exxon-owned oil tanker ran aground and spilled 11 million gallons of oil into one of the pristine sounds situated off the coast of Alaska.[7] This led the U.S. Government to pass the Clean Air and Oil Pollution Acts in 1990, both of which are still in force despite numerous amendments over the last 30 years.

As these regulations increased in frequency, companies' bottom lines suffered, given the expenses needed to follow new rules. Corporations began taking small steps to ameliorate the status quo to avoid these added costs. Simply put, companies would change operational structures to ensure their businesses abided by all relevant regulations, and also made investments to ensure any corporate policies got them ahead of future regulation where possible. In many cases, environmental and other regulatory policies took companies off guard, but those companies with a foresight to plan in advance with proper investments or actions, warded off onerous fees or legal challenges.

---

7. https://www.britannica.com/event/Exxon-Valdez-oil-spill

This process managing regulations was not easy, nor by any means were most companies successful. In some cases, companies identified their own problems that needed regulatory frameworks to help manage, but that was not always feasible either. There is a fine balance between doing the right thing because it's necessary and doing the right thing because the law says so. There are ways for companies to set the parameters, though, to prevent bad things from happening ever again.

Just ask Shayne Tyler.

Shayne says that better business approaches are needed if we are ever to enjoy a trajectory away from shady operations or corrupt handlings. There's a caveat, though. The company, itself, may not always be the one at fault. It could be those ingrained from within that create the greatest challenges. In many cases they provide the best opportunities for growth as well.

Photo courtesy of Shayne Tyler

In 1973, Shayne Tyler was born about 90 miles north of London, in Peterborough, England, a town best known for its 12th- and 13th-century cathedrals with Gothic façades. Shayne calls himself a country boy. His parents were part of the working class; his father plastered walls at building sites while his mother helped raise him and his three brothers and sisters. During Shayne's childhood, happiness was not based on possessions, and he and his siblings were largely left to their own devices. Particularly Shayne.

Shayne was the second of the four children. While his older brother was responsible for looking after the younger Tyler children, Shayne was pretty much able to do as he pleased. He had a curiosity about him that encouraged adventures around town. There was an innate sense that success was important, though, and Shayne's dad reminded him and his siblings that work doesn't come easy. While his dad found odd jobs to add to the family's nest egg, Shayne grew up with a sense that money was tight. His parents did their best to shelter the kids from any challenges, however, and with a sense of purpose, independence, and deliverance, Shayne worked hard as a student in order to succeed as an adult. Shayne never wanted to be a burden to his family.

At 16, Shayne had an inkling to join the army, but was diagnosed with color blindness, ruling out active duty. Instead, Shayne went the route of math. Engineering, while more of interest to him, was off the table as well due to his disability.

During his school holidays, Shayne began working for a food production facility to earn money for his university fees. It was in the late 1980s, and the company was keen to make more money by increasing its yields. It became Shayne's job to find ways to make this company continuously profitable, which he did for the next decade.

When Shayne's employer was sold to a much larger, blue chip food manufacturer, Shayne, now a small fish in a very large pond, felt even more pressure to bring in big profits for management. He progressed up the ranks quickly, using his logic and math skills to make the most decisive moneymaking plans. Shayne says he was a cold decision maker. He relied on logic and numbers, not on the impact of his decisions.

In early 1999, Shayne was offered a position helping one of the largest potato manufacturers in the UK turn itself around from financial struggle. The position was a promotion, and Shayne loved working for this company, especially given his role managing a large team. The job was about big hours and hard work.

Until Shayne's life was changed forever on June 19, 2000, making companies more money was all that mattered.

Unbeknownst to Shayne, the British Broadcasting Company (BBC) had targeted Shayne's company with a news feature on illegal workers. The management got wind that this story would air June 19. Prepared for the worst, and irritated that he would have to manage the blow by the BBC, Shayne woke that same morning to a related column in the newspaper—58 Chinese nationals had been smuggled into the UK from Europe by a labor exploiter. Without sufficient oxygen in the shipping truck they had been piled into, all but two of them died. Their bodies were found at the port of Dover.[8]

Thinking not about the lives of the 56 Chinese laborers, but instead about how this headline would take a toll on his company alongside the BBC exposé, Shayne waited patiently as the BBC shared their findings that evening. They had identified that a labor provider had smuggled workers into the UK and had successfully infiltrated Shayne's company. The laborers were paid £10 a week. Some were making the equivalent of 25 to 30 cents an hour.

It was not uncommon for manufacturing facilities to use additional laborers, especially seasonally (as is still the case to this day), but Shayne's company (and by default, Shayne himself) was complicit in promoting a culture of dependency on laborers, particularly those who were seen as a commodity, possessions in place for a reason, lowest on the totem pole. While the company wasn't intentionally at fault, they certainly weren't doing things right either.

Shayne, as head of operations at the time, had been doing relevant identification checks. No one would have guessed the identification cards, however, were falsified.

---

8. http://news.bbc.co.uk/2/hi/europe/843232.stm

After the BBC program aired, Shayne was aghast to find that the newspaper headlines the next day covered an electricity outage and football game fights instead of this horrific finding. Not to mention the fact that the headlines about the Chinese nationals had long disappeared. Immediately the story didn't have public significance, yet Shayne felt the reality was different. He couldn't believe that the world didn't really care about these laborers, and how one of the largest potato suppliers in the country was complicit through inaction. Shayne was shaken by the normalcy that ensued after the BBC program aired. He realized the problem needed to be addressed. He realized that to be a good business, long-term profitability, while still very important, was perhaps just as important as being ethical and sustainable. Business ethics did not have to come by the way of additional costs.

Shayne began investigating the extent of the exploitation within his company. He found horrendous stories, extreme sexual abuse (one occurrence which led to an illegitimate child), financial larceny, fraud, and terrible treatment of workers. He was in shock, having been raised by his parents to believe that a life is a life, and precious, despite color, creed, background, or upbringing. Shayne could not believe people were being treated so inhumanely. And right under his nose.

Shayne's company ensured the workers were expatriated to their countries and vowed nothing similar would happen again. He stayed another year but was tainted by the experience and needed to move on professionally.

In 2002, Shayne became the operations manager for another food production company, and, on his first day, had to fire the agency supplying factory workers because they were all illegal. Because the UK had a massive shortage of labor, the demand for these laborers was everywhere. With weak legislation to address the challenge of exploited labor, workers came in droves into the UK from all over Europe, the Middle East, and Africa. Agents exploited the workers and manipulated the companies hiring them.

During Shayne's tenure as operations manager between 2002 and 2005, he handled hundreds of cases involving illegal workers. The challenge became personal after his experience in 2000, and he couldn't get over his inability to create a change.

Driven by a fear of failure, no longer the joy of success, no longer the results of profit, Shayne could not bear to look into another victim's eyes knowing their story. For Shayne, and many others during the late 1990s and into the 2000s, being a corporate executive brought with it a much greater sense of responsibility to make changes, to ameliorate wrongdoings, and positively impact society.

Shayne still believes in the role of business to make money. It cannot be denied that we rely on businesses for our basic goods and services. Shayne simply believes that it's also imperative for businesses to be working around the notion of "ethical profit." While Shayne's company had been paying fair wages, it was the exploiters who were preventing the wages from getting to certain workers. The business was not impacted economically in any way by ensuring workers were getting their due wages. Keeping ethical processes in place was just the right thing to do.

In late spring 2005, a female worker informed Shayne that an exploiter had taken her wages. Working with the authorities, which at the time could offer little if any assistance, Shayne tried to investigate on his own. During his investigation, though, he began receiving threats from the trafficker who insisted he knew where Shayne lived and the names of his wife and kids. Shayne felt powerless. Shayne was able to locate and protect seven exploited victims but was unable to secure the safety of another fifty-three. He still feels haunted to this day by their lack of whereabouts.

Feeling a nagging sense of responsibility and lack of action, Shayne realized there was more he could have done. He could have pushed the authorities harder. But he didn't. He was protecting his family first and foremost, as he should. Yet, he hasn't been able to let go of the image of this woman being taken advantage of.

Since 2005, Shayne has made it a personal passion to work with his and other companies to eliminate modern slavery. He continues to face challenges of exploitation more than he would like, but he sees a long-term solution as more legislation is passed to address illegal labor challenges. He also sees promise as companies like Marks & Spencer, a large British retailer Shayne supplies to and works with to enact safe policies, now takes it upon itself to commit to change.

In 2017, Marks & Spencer honored Shayne with an award celebrating his outstanding contribution to sustainability, specifically with regards to his work around modern slavery between the years 2007-2017. Shayne also received the IMPACT award, given by the Gangmasters and Labour Abuse Authority, the UK government's agency working to tackle labor exploitation, for the 18 years of his life he's dedicated to tackling crimes of exploitation.

Shayne still struggles with the missed opportunities of his younger years and the importance he placed on profits, moneymaking, and prestige. He says that one day he'll feel he's done enough. That enough people will take on the challenge of modern slavery so he can rest easy. Until then, Shayne will not give up. He has the full support of his company to fight for those who cannot fight for themselves.

As Shayne shared, those laborers "bleed the same red as anyone else. How dare we judge them for wanting a better life for themselves and their families?"

The corporate culture of the 1980s and 1990s enabled exploitation. And while change is finally happening, it's still slow. It's up to corporate leaders to fight these challenges and be incentivized to do the right thing. Customers are also complicit in driving the ethics of businesses, and they must start recognizing the opportunities to change the status quo with the power of their dollar.

For now, Shayne believes that companies are truly trying to find the secret sauce for doing business in the most sustainable way—while still making money. Businesses must ask themselves how to take available resources and build systems and procedures that allow for safety and equal treatment and fair wages for its laborers. Shayne's company has cracked the nut. The environment of business is dynamic, and there will always be challenges to address, but Shayne is doing everything he can to fight until the paradigm has fully shifted in the right direction.

While regulation was slow to come by in Shayne's experience, it was clear from the public's reactions (or lack thereof) of the BBC exposé, as well as the headlines about the 58 Chinese nationals caught smuggled in Dover, that the stakeholders of these UK companies (i.e. the consumers) were not outraged nor merely interested in the findings.

As the occurrences of mistreated migrant laborers became more prevalent, regulations were enacted, however, and a greater awareness, and thus perception of the correct role for corporate leaders in these situations, took shape. While the real stakeholders of this rampant mistreatment were often ignored (the laborers themselves), the growing attention paid has raised their profile among some of the biggest businesses in the world. Thanks to the work of Shayne and others, businesses worldwide are making decisions for a group of stakeholders that had been ignored for far too long.

As regulations took companies into a new era of responsible practices in the late 1980s and early 1990s, in 1991, a new innovation was taking the world by storm. The World Wide Web became available for public use. Before 1991, scientists, researchers, and technologists were using the Internet to exchange data files. But in 1991, the Internet evolved into a space to share information more broadly and changed our lives forever.

The advent of the Internet meant that information could become more readily available, and many companies were poised to take advantage. It also meant that the world became effectively smaller, as different populated corners were connected by data unlike ever before. Political protests and organized efforts to thwart global environmental and social damage caused by businesses became more commonplace, as the activists found ways to exchange information about actions happening worldwide easier and faster. Globalization became the new symbol of corporate wrongdoings, as many businesses took advantage of information access to tap into new (and often cheaper) labor markets.

The opening of virtual borders became a challenge to many big businesses as customers learned more truths about producing consumer goods, some of which was not positive. Nike, for example, grappled with calls to boycott its shoes after activists found sweatshop conditions in its Indonesia factories.[9] Companies like Avon, Benetton, Hasbro, and Mattel were pressured by PETA (People for the Ethical Treatment of Animals) to stop animal testing as a means to ensure safety for consumer use when news about animal mistreatment pervaded the web.[10] It became clear that practices had to change, or else customers would exit the proverbial front door as fast as they came in.

At the same time brands were warding off negative press or angry customers, a new paradigm was emerging, called "Corporate Social Responsibility," or CSR. There are as many definitions and ways of interpreting CSR as there are businesses that tout their CSR approaches. Ultimately, CSR is most defined as a way of doing business that takes into account environmental, social, and economic impact to all stakeholders. This should include (but does not always) employees, workers, neighbors, customers, investors, local actors, and others who are engaged with a company in some way, shape, or form.

---

9. https://www.theguardian.com/environment/green-living-blog/2012/jul/06/activism-nike

10. https://www.peta.org/about-peta/milestones/

Starting in the 1990s, and still prevalent in these years leading up to 2020, a year that many companies picked as a marker to measure systemic change in their practices, CSR became a driving force for improvements in everything from packaging to energy usage to gender equity considerations to the type of toilet paper used in employee restrooms.

The tricky thing about the evolution of CSR is that some companies legitimately invest in CSR programs because they want to make the right investment decisions, find ways to improve their processes, and investigate more efficient and socially conscious operations. Others sense an imperative to tell a better story than the one they are most known for, and as consumers and other stakeholders become more aware of the misgivings of companies, showcasing CSR as a priority allows companies to ameliorate their less-than-shiny image.

Take the often-chastised Monsanto (recently merged with Bayer). Monsanto, a manufacturer of agricultural chemicals and technologies, also produced consumer products like weed killer Roundup. The company has faced severe criticism in the media for its use of materials deeply dangerous to human health and the environment. In 2018, the company was sued for more than

$280 million by a sufferer of lymphoma claiming it was weed killer that made him so sick.[11] This case was not the first to tarnish Monsanto's image. Many other cases have been made that Monsanto is just out to kill us—literally.

The company produces an annual sustainability report and has since 2012. In its 2017 report, titled "Growing Better Together," the CEO is quoted: "At Monsanto, we're committed to helping create solutions to these challenges while helping to take care of our planet, our people, and the communities where we live and work."[12] The report is broken up into three sections: (1) Better Planet, (2) Better Lives, and (3) Better Partner.

So, is the CEO lying? Are the people who work for Monsanto monsters who want to lie and cheat their way to profitability at the cost of human lives and the detriment of our planet?

As a parent, I am the first to ward off the use of harmful chemicals in my home. I refuse to use Roundup around our lawn. But here's the tricky thing for me, and for a lot of those who work for Monsanto (now Bayer): I do not believe the company is mal-intentioned. I actually do believe the company wants to do better. I know some of the people who work on sustainability for Bayer. They are incredibly kind, dedicated, and honorable people.

---

11. https://www.yahoo.com/news/monsanto-asks-judge-throw-289m-174254482.html

12. https://monsanto.com/app/uploads/2017/12/Sustainability_2017.pdf

The people inside Monsanto or Bayer, and some of the biggest companies in the world, particularly those working on CSR, are trying to improve the way companies do business, and are some of the most talented, dedicated, smart, and empathetic people I know.

I don't discount in any way that there are challenges in the way their products are designed, and I feel tremendous sympathy if those products have hurt people. My guess is that was not the intent of producing a product that was meant to help kill weeds so farmers could grow more healthy vegetables to feed the planet. Yes, money does still talk, and farmers want to sell more, so they can make more. Weed killer helps them do that. But do I believe that the people who created Roundup wanted to harm our health? No. I do not believe that was their intention. I do believe, however, that they have a lot of work to do to turn their product around to be helpful rather than harmful. If you ask the employees at Monsanto or Bayer, they would tell you the same thing.

Those I have met and worked with over the years from Monsanto, Bayer, and companies like Nike, and Avon, and Dow, and Mattel, and Starbucks, and Coca-Cola, and Estee Lauder, and Walmart, and Target, and Chipotle, and General Mills, and frankly any big company that gets bad press on a more-than-often basis, who are among the hundreds or thousands within their companies seeking solutions to our evolving planetary challenges, are GOOD PEOPLE. Most of them have admitted that their companies don't always make the best decisions, or do everything right, and they are deeply disappointed by the harm some of their companies' products or actions have caused. But they are committed to seeing the change that's needed through to fruition.

By no means am I letting these companies off the hook. I simply view those *individuals,* who believe in the power of companies to effect change, are doing what they can within the confines of their companies to do just that. We cannot deny more could be done. But we should consider that efforts to evaluate the social impact role companies can make are underway and are being taken seriously by intelligent, hardworking, caring, and determined individuals.

LESSONS LEARNED: For decades, companies were seen as conglomerates simply out to make money and provide products for consumption. While some of those aims have not changed, the role of business leaders within companies is evolving, and the role of empathy and an interest in improving our planet is shifting the mission of many companies into beacons of social and environmental change. This evolution takes many shapes and sizes, but even the companies with the most challenging history can make progress and effect positive change.

CHAPTER THREE

Beyond Philanthropy: Evolving Corporate Missions

With the realization that companies can do more to improve social, environmental, and economic situations, both locally and globally, some corporate leaders in the 1990s, began strategizing how to play a greater philanthropic role, particularly as regulation and bad press caused sales to falter. Rather than accept brow beating from the nonprofit campaigners, or struggle with never-ending changes in laws or requirements, philanthropy seemed to be a reasonable fix, allowing companies to put their money where their mouth is and invest in charitable causes that make the world better. At the very least this effort would assuage any built-up guilt or feelings of insecurity for those corporate leaders who were questioning whether their company was indeed a steward or a skunk.

The rate of corporate giving skyrocketed between 1990 and the early part of the 21st century accordingly. As noted by *The Chronicle of Philanthropy*, corporate giving was in the hundreds of millions of dollars in 1990. By 2016, corporate philanthropy grew to just under $20 billion.[13] As in "B," "Billion." This figure does not even recognize the billions of dollars companies are investing in improved processes, organizational management, environmentally sustainable technologies, and the like.

Corporate philanthropy did, and still does, take the shape of many types of engagements. In some scenarios, companies give money to a cause important to one of their leaders, or something the employees vote on, like a disease prevention fund or local homeless shelter. Some companies collect funds from their employees for a cause that is near and dear to the company, or encourage their employees to volunteer time to build homes, or serve food at a local pantry. I visited one of our country's biggest retailer headquarters three years ago on a "give back day" and saw how teams of employees were packing school backpacks for underprivileged kids, sewing blankets for homeless veterans, and collecting canned food for a food drive.

Other companies participate in sales-based philanthropy, whereby a percentage of sales goes to a cause

---

13. https://www.philanthropy.com/article/Donations-Grew-14-to-390/240319

that the company believes is necessary to support. This is a particularly effective money-raising tactic for companies that have a strong consumer facing presence, as it allows them to tell their philanthropic story and engage consumers at the same time.

Because of the work I do to help companies evaluate philanthropic partnerships, I was interviewed last year by *Bloomberg Businessweek* about the ways companies and individuals can evolve their philanthropic giving, especially since there is such a high demand among nonprofits for corporate giving dollars. Some of the ideas included setting up scholarships, finding local causes to engage in, and even creating a foundation, something many for-profit companies are considering, both as their efforts to give back grow and philanthropic tax implications change.[14]

The evolution of philanthropy is a book topic in and of itself. The way philanthropy has morphed into CSR and also more business-aligned giving and engagement to address social impact, is evidence of the fact that companies are looking to impact bigger and more critically aligned business issues more than ever before. Being philanthropic is not the same as being a social impact leader, however. Those businesses that have truly ingrained purpose and mission into their way of

---

14. https://www.bloomberg.com/news/features/2017-12-14/how-to-do-nate-to-charity-start-volunteering-do-philanthropy-right

operating are doing more than giving away money or time. They are learning slowly that their role in this ever-changing world is pivotal to making the world better through their day-to-day business decision making, not just by writing a check.

ArcelorMittal is the world's largest steel and mining company. With nearly 200,000 employees, operations in 60 countries, and production of more than 113 million tons of steel per year,[15] one would not assume Arcelor-Mittal is leading efforts to improve the planet. In fact, as a former steel town girl, I always assume companies like ArcelorMittal are blowing black smoke from factories around the world, taking advantage of low-income workers, and saving money for glass-enclosed corner offices among the c-suite. Like many assumptions we make without doing our due diligence, all of this would be wrong. In fact, ArcelorMittal communicates this message front and center on their website.

Portions of text from their sustainability page read:

---

15. https://corporate.arcelormittal.com/who-we-are/at-a-glance

Excerpts from ArcelorMittal's website

Rising to the sustainability challenge

Steel has a vital role to play in creating a sustainable future, and as the world's largest steel and mining company, we know that, as well as opportunities, this brings with it huge challenges.

Sustainability is all about taking a long-term perspective, and that's what we already do as a business....

Global challenges and opportunities

The world faces enormous challenges in the 21st century: from climate change to increasing pressures on natural resources; from the lifestyle expectations of those in the developed world, to tackling poverty at the base of the pyramid in emerging markets. These issues have a direct impact on businesses, as well as governments, civil society, and individuals. And businesses face other challenges, including the growing expectation that they should report more openly, act more responsibly, protect the environment, and support their local communities. All of these factors pose risks to companies as large as ours—risks to our profits, reputation, operations, and social license to operate, if we fail to manage them. But they also present us with enormous opportunities, from the commercial potential of new greener products, to the innovation potential of a new generation of people entering our industry.

We have the power to make a positive difference to our stakeholders and shareholders, as well as society as a whole. In order to do this, we need to address the risks and opportunities arising from social and environmental trends across our operations. We must also use our knowledge of the impacts of steel to persuade our customers—and their consumers—to make and choose products that are more sustainable.

Our 10 sustainable development outcomes

We are developing a new sustainable development framework around the outcomes that will help us secure the commercial success of our business in the medium term, while contributing to solving the world's sustainable development challenges in the long term. This is good for society, good for our stakeholders, and good for us.

The language is pretty powerful stuff coming from a steel and mining conglomerate. It's honest. It's believable. It's even inspiring. The text allows the reader to feel connected, and it makes me think that Arcelor-Mittal is truly considering its stakeholders (consumers, community members, employees, and yes, absolutely shareholders) in its business actions.

These commitments are far reaching, but crucial as they show the undertaking of a very big company that is willing to do what is necessary to shape the world in a positive way. They show that the time for pure money-making behavior is behind us. It's time to act, and act in a positive way. The decisions to do so are not easy and are weighed with precision. It takes someone like Marcy Twete, ArcelorMittal's former Executive Director of Corporate Responsibility, to focus leadership on why a positive influence is so critical for a company like theirs.

Photo courtesy of Marcy Twete

A town of just 5,000 people, Devils Lake, North Dakota, where Marcy grew up, is made up of rural farmland and beautiful countryside. Marcy comes from a very large and closely connected family (in proximity and relationship). Marcy didn't travel much in her early childhood, just to Minnesota and back to visit with family members. Her dad worked for the local, rural telephone company, which was bought out when Marcy was in second grade. Transferred to St. Louis for her father's new job, Marcy learned about the "outside" world. She experienced for the first time, diversity, accessibility, economic division, and racial divides. She was fasci nated by this world, one that seemed big and new and full of opportunities to learn.

After two years in St. Louis, the family moved to Montana where Marcy's father took up a new job. But soon enough they landed back in Devil's Lake.

While growing up in this small town, Marcy felt agitated and impatient. She wanted to get out and see the world. She left Devil's Lake at 17 and never looked back.

Attending a small school outside of Minneapolis and majoring in political science, Marcy had an opportunity to intern in Washington, D.C. In many ways Marcy found her true self—personally and professionally—in D.C. She saw that the outside world she found originally in St. Louis was in need of someone like her to guide policies and action. She realized that making a difference in the world was everything.

Rather than attend law school, one of Marcy's professors encouraged her to find roles within the nonprofit community in order to work for greater purpose. That she did.

For eight years, Marcy worked for nonprofits, finding a rise to leadership that provided her with great personal development. While working with big companies at her nonprofit, she learned about fundraising and philanthropy, she engaged with boards, and saw women leaders making grand commitments within companies that inspired her. She created lofty goals for herself and set her sights on working for a high-powered corporation.

Marcy landed at ArcelorMittal, taking a role as Executive Director for Corporate Responsibility in the Americas. Having worked with corporate responsibility leaders for most of her career from the nonprofit side, she had a good sense of what the role might entail—the fantastic and the terrible. Marcy took the reins as the company had built an already strong responsibility practice, but the opportunity was there to take the program from good to great. It's unrealistic to show up at a facility and eliminate carbon emissions immediately, however. Nor can leadership be convinced to spend hundreds of millions of dollars on a paradigm-shifting program without understanding the consequences and opportunities. ArcelorMittal was devoted to making the changes necessary, nonetheless, in order to position itself in a more positive light within its communities.

Within five years, Marcy and her team were doing fantastic work creating public-private-partnerships that would positively impact community economic development by implementing a world-wide sustainability narrative. This narrative was one of the most forward looking in the steel industry, and was externally lauded. Marcy felt their work truly changed the game for ArcelorMittal, and the industry as a whole.

When one works for a major industrial company, with presence in nearly every corner of the world, it is nearly impossible to ignore some of the negative consequences of corporate investments. Some of the ArcelorMittal projects had been in operation for hundreds of years. Marcy did have moments when she saw some of that negative impact, but she viewed her role as the change maker and sought to find a better way. Big changes take time. But the willingness was there, and that's one of the most important drivers of change.

What Marcy did focus on was developing the best practices for engaging stakeholders in the communities where ArcelorMittal worked and operated, so she could build an understanding of the challenges at play, learn about what solutions were possible, educate her leadership, and be a good neighbor for the communities around ArcelorMittal at the same time. She made it a priority to do the best she could to turn the ship, recognizing a really big ship turns really slowly. Patience and empathy to recognize what changes were needed was everything.

As Marcy explained, in any corporation, big, small, global, or local, there are walls and barriers that prevent sustainability leaders from getting their jobs done. A lot of those barriers are about dollars and cents, and that cannot be ignored. In a company that is very old guard and very traditional male and white, cutting through the narrative of climate change, social progress, or "tree hugging initiatives" is very difficult. ArcelorMittal exists, however, so we can drive a car, and run a washing machine, and sit on bleachers at a stadium because its steel makes it all possible.

Marcy made incredible progress developing a sustainability narrative despite the limitations, as the programs were broad enough to inspire people in different ways and deep enough to move the company forward. She had small wins, like seeing a leader, who had never bought into sustainability, taking her talking points about the importance of ArcelorMittal as a corporate steward to a meeting and championing her work. And she had big wins that were slow and hard fought. In one small town, a well-known environmental activist said to Marcy about ArcelorMittal, "I like you guys. I wish you weren't here. But I like you." In a perfect world, perhaps ArcelorMittal wouldn't have a facility in some of the rural towns where activists prefer there was no such facility, but, in the end, the company was a good partner, and the community valued that immensely.

After five years with ArcelorMittal, Marcy left the company following her graduation from Kellogg's Executive MBA program. She is looking forward to bringing her passion for sustainability and societal change into the next phase of her career in a business that believes being a good citizen is just as much a part of being a business as making money.

Marcy shared that very few companies in the world do sustainability well enough to truly move the needle. For real systemic change, Marcy sees a need for social, environmental, and economic improvement values to be "baked" into the way of doing business, not just part of a philanthropic division or series of projects. The companies that truly get this, and that are doing it well, have leaders in the c-suite who know that long-term sustainability *for* the business (i.e. making a lot of money) is about having long-term sustainability *in* the business (i.e. investing in social and environmental stewardship in a smart and thoughtful way). She believes that a sustainability leader should find the best possible way to imbed him or herself into the core business units, so sustainability is just as much about running a business as any other factor.

Marcy reveres Michael Dell. He makes a lot of money. So do his shareholders. But he has ruthlessly ensured that Dell is as much about making a lot of money as it is about being sustainable. As Marcy reminded me, he sat on a live stage and actually ate his own plant-based packaging. He claims that Dell is about driving value—financial value, shareholder return, and also doing right by doing good.

SAP's Bill McDermott is another leader who gets it right at every turn, according to Marcy. He believes in the power and importance of the Sustainable Development Goals (SDGs) as a guide for business to act more responsibly. He views SAP as a service provider to make people better off in society as a whole.

As for Marcy herself, when she becomes CEO (not if, but when) she would like to fix the epidemic of short-term reporting. The quarter-to-quarter reporting structure many companies use does not allow for long-term sustainability planning. She will also invest in corporate leaders who have experienced the world, and who understand the global interconnectedness that makes corporations critical citizens of an always-dynamic world. This she values particularly after making the journey herself. She wants to do away with the "us vs. them" mentality and break down barriers so we can all work together in a productive way. She knows the value businesses can bring to society. Businesses exist to make money. But they also can and should exist to make the world better.

Corporates have long struggled with what that role looks like. In other words, how will they go about making the world better than it is? Is making edible packaging enough? Will being a good corporate citizen by being a good neighbor to those located in their community do the trick? How does a company determine what element within that company makes it truly possible to make the world better?

One argument often shared about the evolution of philanthropy and CSR in corporates is that in order to make a real difference in the world, employees must belong to the mission, feel a part of the difference making, and be involved in decision making around which causes to support. Certainly engaging employees is one way of completely imbedding sustainability within a company's business.

According to *Forbes*[16] analysis on Cone Communications' 2017 CSR Study, letting employees lead around social and environmental sustainability issues from within helps a company evolve into a true sustainability leader. This goes beyond being purely philanthropic. It's identifying ways for company employees to feel vested in the future of the company and not just "what it stands for...but what it stands up for."[17]

By listening to employees, companies gain varied and diverse perspectives, and learn from within about the ways to address the needs and interests of stakeholders outside their four walls, outside their glass-enclosed offices, and outside even their own communities.

Volunteer days, humanitarian trips, fundraisers, cause competitions, crowdfunding, even exchanges between staff (i.e., staff from corporations spend time working with nonprofit partners for a set period of time, and nonprofit employees spend time working within the corporations for a set period of time) can teach a company a lot about what the "outside world" looks like, smells like, feels like, and acts like. An effort to find the emotions from inside a company, and build

---

16. https://www.forbes.com/sites/glennllopis/2018/02/05/reinventing-philanthropy-as-an-employee-centered-growth-strategy/#-579becf37a5a

17. http://www.conecomm.com/research-blog/2017-csr-study#download-the-research

lessons from the outside into the plans on the inside, makes turning an older, rusty, and one-dimensional ship into a stalwart, thoughtful, and forward-looking titan of change.

LESSONS LEARNED: When companies recognize that there are other needs outside of the philanthropic domain for their active engagement, and they take ownership of their role to steer the ship in a direction of positive change, making the world a better place is not only possible, it's inevitable.

CHAPTER FOUR

Perspective and Passion: Empathetic Mindsets and Sympathetic Hearts

If you look hard enough at peoples' faces, particularly into their eyes, you can see the moment when an experience resonates within the deepest part of their hearts. You can tell from that moment that being in the present has become more than about learning, or being, but entirely about feeling.

During the times I have traveled with corporate leaders to communities that are tied to their company, but happen to be thousands of miles away (think of the farmers that grow beans for a soup mix, the factory workers that sew the laces that tie our running shoes, or the scrap sifters who look through metal and iron to find the materials we need to make our cell phones work), I see in their eyes that transformation from thinking to feeling.

They may originally take on the experience as an attempt to check a box. Perhaps their boss or Board have asked them to visit a supplier and check the status of a product line. Or they were encouraged to visit a community to learn more about how it operates, either to improve a process, or potentially court new consumers. Whatever the reason for bringing corporate leaders into the "field," the results are almost always extraordinary. Hearts take over minds. And the real role of business becomes clear. It is not just about money. It's about the families. The children. The villages they visit.

Erin O'Hara is the Marketing Director for Numi Tea. Headquartered in Oakland, California, Numi Tea's vision is to "inspire well-being of mind, body, and spirit through the simple art of tea." The company is not shy about its priorities of "celebrating people, planet, and tea," and thus it's no surprise that the company's work is very focused on its social impact and environmental sustainability. The company is also growing like gangbusters. It's a leading importer of organic, Fair Trade tea[18] in North America, and as its sales skyrocket, larger

---

18. http://fortune.com/2013/10/31/numi-organic-teas-brother-and-sister-brewers/

brands are taking notice. In 2016, Smucker's and Numi signed a licensing agreement for iced tea ready-to-drink beverages, elevating its status as a major player in the beverage space.

Photo courtesy of Erin O'Hara, Numi Tea

In May 2018, Erin traveled to Wuyuan, China, where Numi sources organic tea for its Jasmine Green from a partner cooperative of 12 years. Erin shared her experience in a Numi blog titled "Why CommuniTea Matters." Her experience in her own words:

> *"You can travel to a different country and a different place—miles and worlds away, full of different sights, sounds, tastes, and smells, but there is always a connection that can be made, a collective understanding among complete strangers through universal truths.*

As a working mother of two young children, it had been a long time since I experienced a trip that ignited such inspiration and wonder.

I remember it was hot and muggy, and the mist that was clinging to the mountainous hills was burning off.

I walked up a steep muddy path from the gates of the factory, side by side with the workers. All of them are women, carrying baskets to collect the harvest with hands weathered from picking for so many years. Smooth, but creased with storied experience. I find out through an interpreter that one of the women has been working here for 10 years. I study her hands and think about how I have surely had a cup of tea from the leaves she once plucked. That single connection suddenly becomes a defining and profound moment for me. Don't get me wrong, I enjoy my weekend farmers' market visits, but there is something wild and completely humbling about meeting this farmer, halfway across the world from where I usually enjoy my cup of tea. I watch as her hands move harmoniously, plucking the top two leaves and the bud. She moves as if conducting a symphony. Her basket is soon half filled. And all I am left with is gratitude. She is the origin, and I am the ending.

I am...here to film the story about connection to...impact...a story of people thriving and success at multiple levels. And as that story becomes apparent, a deeper, more interesting story emerges for me: one of true friendship.

Mr. Hong, chairman of [the cooperative], and Brian, Numi's president who once led all of our sourcing relationships, have now known each other for many years. I can see it in the way they interact. They do not speak the same language, but the formality of business and strangers is not there. It is comfortable and familiar. It is in the way that Mr. Hong's family joins us for dinner each night. It is that Mrs. Hong harvested vegetables in her garden and gifted me a cucumber. It is the ability to all share a laugh together when Brian blasts Al Green from his phone and enjoys an impromptu dance with one of the pluckers. It is spending an hour of zen helping Mr. Hong weed the terraced rows of tea bushes....

It starts to rain. It turns from a few drops to a deluge in a matter of minutes. These women are pros though. They pull out their umbrellas and plastic rain covers like I am sure they have done hundreds of times before...We make our way back to the factory to wait out the storm. While we sit and wait, I notice that they have smart phones. A tale of modernity, income equality, and a thriving economy. I catch the image of children on one of the women's phone and try to charade my way into asking how old her children are. I pull out my phone and share the pictures of my girls. We both make "ohh" and "ahh" sounds as we share our pictures. Not needing to speak Chinese, or her English, we understand that we share the bond of motherhood. Our hopes and worries are similar for that fact alone. Wanting the best for our children and working hard to ensure that we give them all the opportunities we can. Balancing it all. We see each other.

The tea factory manager...lives on site with his family, in a small apartment off the back. Tonight is special, as one of his daughters recently had a baby. The expression on his face when he sees his grandchild is nothing but pure joy. They are having a big family dinner tonight to celebrate all being together, and the energy in the air is sweet and buzzing with love and excitement. It is special indeed to witness such a tender moment.

I learn that [the factory manager's] daughter grew up here. The work he has done in his time as farm manager has provided well for his family. He was able to send his daughter to University and off into the big world. The bright story here is that she has decided to return, to use her education to help further the business. This is a rare story these days, as farming is tougher to do, and higher incomes mean that people are choosing new careers in urban areas. Sharing your craft and watching your children grow into something you helped build must be incredible.

One of the best highlights of the trip was visiting a school. Using the funds from the Fair Trade collective, a school dormitory was built. A picture of the building has even been featured on the back of our box.

With only a couple hours to visit, we jumped right in with the kids. We were a delightful disruption for many of the classrooms: skipping to the front of the room to say hello, playing basketball in the courtyard, and practicing the few Chinese words we had picked up, which ended up as an eruption of laughs.

The experience of being there, holding the hands of these kids as we ran around in a circle, was a beautiful reminder of why brands like Numi and programs like Fair Trade are so important. To see a community that is thriving, from the top owner, to the farmers and workers, and to their families and friends, shows how vital a few extra pennies and a bit of humanity and care truly are. No doubt we need a little more of that these days."

Erin's passion, enthusiasm, and appreciation for the role Numi plays in engaging with the tea communities are obvious. As an employee and leader within the company, being able to capture the emotions, the images, and the experience, and share internally, but also to Numi's stakeholders through its blog, is a gift. Additionally, standing side-by-side tea pickers, and celebrating moments of humanity, like sharing pictures of children, makes the world a much smaller place, and the connections between those working for Numi inside its four walls, and those outside the four walls, much closer and stronger.

One visit I made to Guatemala in 2014 was particularly moving in a similar way and showed me the importance of leaders like Erin experiencing "other worlds" that are still very much relevant to a company's decision making.

I joined several corporate leaders on a trip to review a project in which their companies had invested. As part of the trip, we joined one of their nonprofit partners to visit a recipient of some of the corporations' funding.

We drove for hours from Guatemala City, and trekked up muddy roads to visit a family in the middle of the hills near the Mexican border. We met with a husband

and wife, just 40, but whose faces showed years of hardship. The woman, Magdalena, had given birth to seven children, now ages eight to 21. She had no teeth, but a wide smile. Magdalena showed us around her very modest home. She had a tin roof and one small sleeping room, where she, her husband, and five of their seven children slept. Their bathroom was outside in the fields, and their kitchen was an outdoor room covered by a tarp. This way of living is very common in this part of the world. These families are quite poor, and their means are limited. Still, though, Magdalena had a pride about her.

Photo of Magdalena and her husband
courtesy of Joanne Sonenshine

She had made us a local dish of masa corn meal and steamed greens called boxbol. She asked us to sit down in the plastic chairs the nonprofit had brought into the kitchen. Serving the corporate leaders first, and then me, she smiled, saying in Spanish that she had little to share, but felt happy she could make us a meal. I glanced to my left and saw these corporate leaders, all women, very moved and taken by Magdalena. They were honored, dismayed, and grateful all at once. These leaders had had experiences like this before. But still, seeing their hearts feel such gratitude in concert with Magdalena's pride in serving us and sharing a meal, made me recognize how terribly important it is for corporate decision makers to see for themselves who benefits from corporate philanthropy. Additionally, it is pivotal for corporate leaders to take these experiences back to their companies and share with others, which these leaders did through blog writing and sharing pictures both with colleagues and the public at large.

For many companies, finding ways to engage employees, particularly leaders, in experiences like the one we had in Guatemala, is becoming increasingly common. New companies have sprung up that create humanitarian, philanthropic, or learning trips so individuals can experience the other half of the world, and understand the differences around us. I've listed a few of these companies in the back of this book for your reference.

Learning and "origin" missions are not to pat each other on the back about the amount of money given to a charity, working on community development, or to force an experience that some may not be ready for, but instead to provide employees a way to think creatively about tapping into other consumer bases, or prospective employees for overseas facilities, or to determine what types of programs a company should fund as part of its work in rural development. These trips are meant to teach and allow for experience. They are pivotal for companies trying to be profitable and purposeful at the same time.

In addition to identifying opportunities for a company to learn and grow and innovate by understanding communities where it has a presence, exploring the world allows individuals to experience life in such a different way than sitting in an office. Travel, exploration, learning about other ways of living or cultures, and different approaches to work gives us a shot in the arm of humanity. It forces us to question our intuition and our sense of comfort. It pushes us to think about things, places, and people other than ourselves. American writer Henry Miller once said, "One's destination is never a place, but a new way of seeing things."

It should be noted that in this day and age (late 2018 at time of writing) experiencing "other worlds" need not involve travel or high expense. In addition to the abundance of information available on the Internet, virtual reality is becoming a critical tool for businesses to work on prototyping, or view a new corporate location, or communicate with overseas colleagues.

Using virtual reality to get a sense for how other communities live is only expanding in practice, and can be a great tool for businesses and its stakeholders to build upon their understanding of other cultures, other parts of the world where they may want to invest, or even communities in their own backyard.

I experienced one company using virtual reality to help tell its social impact story to an audience at a conference this year. This Bar Saves Lives is a line of snack and nutrition bars made of yummy ingredients like chocolate, coconut, cherries, and pecans. For every bar sold, the company donates one nutrient packet (a peanut butter-type product that helps malnourished children get much needed vitamins and minerals) to children suffering from malnourishment in places like Haiti, Uganda, and South Sudan.

The company's website states that while the snack bars are delicious, the ultimate aim of the company is not about making snack bars. It is really about ending childhood malnutrition worldwide. The company is only a few years old but has already made a difference in thousands of children's lives, helping them grow and thrive in difficult circumstances.

I had heard about This Bar Saves Lives before visiting their booth at the conference, when I read about one of its co-founders in *Fast Company*. He had been named one of the "Most Creative People in Business" by the magazine because of the way he had courted big retailers like Whole Foods, Target, and Starbucks to carry the bars. One of the company's campaigns, "This Workplace Saves Lives" called for big companies like Google and LinkedIn to start providing bars to its employees as well, thus amplifying the number of bars the company could donate. Ryan Devlin, the co-founder profiled was quoted as saying: "We named our company This Bar Saves Lives, which everyone said was insane...Now, that's our number-one asset."

At the conference, This Bar Saves Lives had a beautifully designed booth with vibrant images of the bars (and the bright colored and inviting packaging), but also with pictures of exuberant children from all over the world. The company's mission was made abundantly clear in this display.

Near the booth, the company had set up a virtual reality station, where attendees and retail buyers could put on a VR set and be transported to the communities where This Bar Saves Lives provides nutrient packs. It was uplifting to see how individuals responded to the experience, literally being taken to the villages and experiencing firsthand the need for companies like This Bar Saves Lives to make the investments they are making. Being transferred into that world was monumental and allowed participants to engage emotionally with the product. It was both moving and brilliant by This Bar Saves Lives to utilize the VR technology to transplant potential customers and encourage their engagement and connection.

Todd O'Rourke lives This Bar Saves Lives' mission as the company's Co-Founder. He notes, *"This Bar Saves Lives is a mission first company. We started the company out of our desire to end a global crisis. We also always knew that we would only be successful if our product is great, too. So, we focus on providing the healthiest, most delicious bars while also having the biggest impact on the malnutrition crisis. We have found that if you let passion for a mission drive your company, it can only lead to success on every front."*

Indeed, what is similar between Erin's story, my experience in Guatemala, and the work of This Bar Saves Lives, is that all of the leaders behind the brands had a natural predisposition to empathy. For Erin, she felt the emotional connection to the women tea pickers and the children around her, as well as the beautiful land growing her company's product. To the corporate leaders with me in Guatemala, they had the ability to empathize with Magdalena, and encourage her by enjoying her efforts to prepare us a meal. For the founders of This Bar Save Lives, it was a trip to a refugee camp in Liberia in 2009, where they encountered many malnourished children in desperate need of life-saving nutrition. Their empathy propelled them to find a solution that could provide long lasting and sustainable nutrition products to these and many other children.

Empathy is not the same as sympathy, just like being a social impact leader in business is not the same as being purely philanthropic. Merriam-Webster defines empathy as "the action of understanding, being aware of, being sensitive to, and vicariously experiencing the feelings, thoughts, and experience of another of either the past or present without having the feelings, thoughts, and experience fully communicated in an objectively explicit manner."

Sympathy is defined in a number of ways, but most generally by this definition: "The act or capacity of entering into or sharing the feelings or interests of another."

To be sympathetic means you are able to share the feelings of others. Being empathetic, however, is about understanding others' feelings, and recognizing those feelings, without having them yourself.

Here's an example: When one of your friends loses a loved one, you feel their sorrow, literally. Feeling sympathy you may cry with them, your heart hurts hearing about their loss. You share their feelings literally. With empathy, your heart may feel a certain emotion strongly, but it is not the same emotion as the recipient.

For Erin, she felt empathy toward the tea growers because she was inspired and moved by their hard work and dedication to the craft of growing tea. But she did not feel their same feelings. That would be almost impossible. Erin is not living in China and picking tea. Thus, she can experience emotional thoughts toward them, without having the same feelings that they possess.

The nuance is important. Being an empathetic leader in business means you are able to feel strongly toward a specific cause or approach that has an emotional pull from within. It means that along with deep thinking, decision-making involves an understanding of what others experience, and thus investments in social and environmental impact programs are made through a lens of that understanding.

Being a sympathetic leader means you feel sad or sorry or emotional about a certain situation, cause, or effort. But you aren't making decisions grounded in those emotions. Thus, philanthropy allows a sympathetic leader to give support and assuage a feeling. Imbedding social impact into decision making at the highest level, however, means that empathy will drive how businesses operate, not just one-off philanthropic actions.

Now don't get me wrong, both empathy and sympathy are critical in business. But the distinction is really important. Making changes in society that are lasting will not be met through philanthropy alone. There is simply not enough money in philanthropy to shift the true development paradigm. Having lasting change will only be possible if businesses imbed empathetic action into their decision making, just as Erin, the team at This Bar Saves Lives, and the leaders I was with in Guatemala have done.

There is a ton of data out there about the correlation between empathy in leadership and employee retention and profitability (high empathy does reward itself in terms of revenues, or so it seems). It's no accident that a company like Numi is selling its tea fast and furiously. People these days want to support companies that are "doing the right thing" for the most part, as long as it doesn't cost too much. More on that conundrum later.

As more leaders use their natural empathetic skills, or even if they have to learn it (indeed, you can now take trainings in empathy), decision making in business is evolving from being just about the money, to being about what's right.

LESSONS LEARNED: Gaining awareness and exposure to the world around us is what makes us the most effective at changing the world and passing that value on within our four walls will drive the agenda farther. Empathy is a critical skill in business to ensure change is coming from a place of true meaning and consideration of needs outside one's own perspective.

CHAPTER FIVE

Connections and Influence: Purpose Creation and Actionable Commitments

As part of my master's program, I wrote and defended my thesis titled: *Globalization and Growth: How Information Flows Affect GDP Per Capita*. At the time (2002), the Internet was fully developed, but access was still an issue. Rather than examine Internet access, therefore, I tested correlations between telephone technology (i.e. land lines) and economic development. This allowed me to analyze access in some of the more remote areas of the globe. Unsurprisingly, a higher rate of telephone usage (and more precisely, the number of telephone lines available to a community) translated to a higher Gross Domestic Product (GDP).

While I knew my thesis was not revolutionary, or even unique, it proves an important point that is still relevant. The more information available, the more opportunities exist to leverage knowledge for economic advancement. Having more insight into how individuals may respond to marketing, price points, or other forms of engagement has changed how companies interact with consumers and other stakeholders at an accelerated pace, no matter where they are in the world at any given time.

This accessibility puts pressure on companies to be almost everywhere at once and be everything to everyone. They must make good products, provide an excellent level of service, and also invest in employee engagement and internal operations, processes, etc. It's no wonder that many companies scoff at the added responsibility and cost of investing in other programs that seem just "nice to have."

The realization that many companies have made, however, is that these "outside" programs are way more than "nice to have." They are indeed critical for many consumers that prioritize this level of commitment to issues other than making money. This is especially true of generations younger than mine. There are more articles and research studies than one could possibly read about the way millennials and even younger generations make purchasing decisions. It's undeniable that companies are responding to the trend in appealing to the smartphone generations that believe social goodness is integral.

In an article[19] I co-wrote on the topic of millennials changing the shape of sustainability, I opined around my uncertainty that generational trends matter.

I questioned whether these consumers are taking the risks required to reshape the economy in a way that will truly move business in a different direction. Does the desire for purpose really lead to action? Do businesses really prioritize the "doing good" aspects of their work to respond to consumer shifts? If the way businesses are responding to the subtle push tells us anything, I'd say the answer is "yes!"

As an example, toward the end of 2018, I co-authored a paper about the role of corporations in helping small-holder farmers in remote, developing economies, earn a higher living income. By interviewing over 20 organizations that engage with companies on a regular basis to address major global challenges, there was an incredible variance In responses to the question about the role companies play in making the world a better place. Some organizations we interviewed saw many of the problems the global poor face today being directly attributed to imbalances of power between global corporations and the underserved populations in the most rural parts of the world. Others saw companies as merely out to take advantage of the poorest of the poor, seeing them purely

---

19. https://www.triplepundit.com/2017/10/next-generation-ready-sustain-ability-challenge/

as workers, and not as potential business partners (my bias is to the latter, as I see a huge untapped world of potential business partners in the developing world. It just so happens that those potential business partners can also be very viable consumers if given the right access, finance, and funding). Still others indeed saw companies responding to the consumers' push to do better, be better, and lead better.

Companies obviously play a unique role in addressing issues like poverty alleviation or other development challenges, particularly if they have large market share or far reach. They have decision-making authority that many of those entities that they engage with down the chain simply don't. This presents a conundrum, since many companies have the ability to exert influence on a range of other powerful actors, including suppliers, governments, and end consumers. They also have a vested interest in the future of their business, and when growth depends on individuals on the other side of the world, there is a role that companies may need to play to ensure those individuals are thriving and have a future. Otherwise the chain may be broken as individuals leave factories, farms, processing facilities, etc., and head to city centers looking for more lucrative work. Seeing the chain break leads many consumers to other brand allegiances in some cases.

This does not mean that companies should be responsible for shifting every paradigm for every one of their stakeholders, however. Instead, companies must think about the systems they are a part of and contribute to, depend upon, work in and around, source from, and work with. Local contexts matter, and the interconnectedness of our planet makes it unavoidable for companies to ignore the realities of living and working in different parts of the world, where challenges, opportunities, lifestyles, and traditions differ. If a company wants to source a product, or build a factory, or hire employees from Africa, for example, it will be a very different context than doing the same in Spain.

The story of Pierrette Djemain, the founder of Plantes Aromatiques des Collines (PAC) in Benin, highlights how even the most ancillary support (in this case from a U.S. Peace Corps business training) can help propel someone's life, career, and opportunity, and allow them to be profitable in their business. It shows how mission and success go hand in hand. Pierrette, and the companies to which she supplies, take making profits as seriously as they do giving back to her community.

Photo of Pierrette Djemain courtesy of Plantes Aromatiques des Collines (PAC)

Pierrette Djemain was born in a village called Gnidjazoun, in the commune of Bohicon, about an hour and a half from Dassa-Zoumé, Benin, where she currently lives. One of 12 children (all still alive today), Pierrette grew up in Ivory Coast, in a town called Yamoussoukro. Her father served in the army before she was born, while her mother took care of the children. Upon completion of his service, Pierrette's father became a farmer.

For the first five years of her life, Pierrette recalls going back and forth between her village in Benin and Yamoussoukro. In addition to farming, Pierrette's father performed a series of odd jobs, and once the children were old enough, her mother took a job buying merchandise (mostly clothes and shoes) in large quantities and re-selling them to local villagers for a profit. Of little means, her parents did everything they could to make sure Pierrette and her siblings had enough food to eat and were in good enough health.

Pierrette finished three grades of primary school in Yamoussoukro before moving back to Benin for good. The teachers in Benin did not believe the education standards were as high in Ivory Coast at the time, so Pierrette had to start school over again upon moving. She spent another two years in school before she faced some societal pressures around the notion of girls not belonging in school with boys. Pierrette's father supported Pierrette leaving school, even though her mother was not fond of the idea. Regardless, while all of her brothers stayed in school through university levels, Pierrette helped her mother sell clothes and shoes in the village instead. She was 11 years old.

Pierrette's parents separated shortly thereafter, and several years later, she and her mother moved in with Pierrette's aunt. One day, Pierrette's mother went to retrieve some of their belongings back in Ivory Coast. She was gone for two months, and soon Pierrette learned that she had died.

Pierrette continued to buy and sell clothes and other household merchandise with her aunt. Her aunt would travel to other villages for three or four days at a time, sell her wares, and return. Leaving a full stock of merchandise behind, Pierrette's aunt left for Cotonou in Benin, leaving behind the merchandise for Pierrette to sell, sending all money onwards to her aunt. It was incredibly tough for her to survive on her own.

Around the age of 17, Pierrette met a man who would become her husband. Needing someone to support her, Pierrette married the man and began having children soon thereafter. Entirely dependent on her husband, Pierrette was left completely bereft when, pregnant with her fifth child, her husband died. Pierrette's husband's family tried to force a marriage with her late husband's brother (who already had one wife), and when she refused, they disowned her. She was truly alone, since her husband's family was all she had, and she struggled to support her five children with no money, no education, and no future.

Going house-by-house asking for small jobs, washing clothes, or folding sheets, Pierrette woke up each morning worried about how she would support her children.

One day Pierrette signed up for a Peace Corps-sponsored training supported by the U.S. Government's Feed the Future food security initiative, training women on how to process moringa, a green, leafy plant that when dried and ground, can be used as a powerful supplement to meals and drinks due to its high nutrient density.

While moringa powder is highly sought after in Benin due to its health benefits, it can be expensive and sometimes contaminated. Pierrette realized in this training that she could make money for her family and work with her community by starting a business making the highest quality, most affordable moringa powder in the region. Moringa grows fast, so it was easy to find, and she used the skills she recalled from working with her father in the fields to cultivate and process the leaves.

Over the next two years, Pierrette started building a network of households in her community to whom she would teach planting and pruning techniques. Although she could have planted her own trees to reduce costs, Pierrette's vision was to engage her community and build a method of development that went beyond her own needs. By purchasing leaves from others, Pierrette was able to provide her moringa growers with financial stability.

Pierrette organized and trained women who were widows, struggling to make ends meet, to process the moringa leaves into powder. She wanted the women to feel ownership of the company and play an important role in the development of the business. She wanted them to feel useful.

Starting the business with only 1,000 francs (about $2.00) was tough. Pierrette didn't have much of a market to sell to, or even a firm understanding of the processing. But little by little, Pierrette's company grew. Plantes Aromatiques des Collines (PAC), Pierrette's business, now sells to 25 different retail locations around Central Benin.

Pierrette claims that it was the financial support and encouragement from other business owners and organizations she's encountered during her journey, who understood and valued her mission, that kept her going, and allowed her to stay positive despite her financial and personal challenges. While her company is still small, it is growing.

Pierrette believes real success will come when she can access much bigger markets. All that said, already she can see the fruits of her labor. Representatives from outside of Benin have come to see her and to visit her operations, particularly as the moringa plant gains in popularity in the United States and other western countries. She is hopeful that this will translate to more sales. The foreign visitors appreciate the way Pierrette has buoyed women farmers, and how she provides consistent-paying jobs to the local communities. That can only mean that these matters of importance to her, women's empowerment and a sense of pride and independence, are values to others as well, which she finds encouraging.

Pierrette believes that she was put on this Earth to help those who have been disadvantaged by life. She has empathy (her words, not mine) for those going through tough times. She sees opportunities to create economic advances for the vulnerable, (widows, orphans, forgotten women) by planting moringa trees, revitalizing the environment, and developing a value chain that provides entire families with a resilient source of income.

When Pierrette was young, her mother suffered through many hardships. Pierrette always assumed she would finish school, get a job, and help other women, so they could be saved from the trauma that her mother faced. But then she experienced hardships herself. She's always imagined that there are a lot of women who have similar challenges, and it's her dream to help those women. Pierrette never imagined she would do so as an entrepreneur.

When I asked Pierrette through a translator over a shaky WhatsApp connection about what advice she may give to big corporate CEOs, she said that she sees a lot of business owners and leaders working to enrich themselves even if all around them there are people suffering, poor, and disadvantaged. She continued that it's indeed possible to earn a lot of money in business. But if the "people around you are poor, you are still poor, too."

Pierrette believes that the objective of business at its core is to improve society—"That's the true richness."

Pierrette's story is one that should inspire anyone working in business to seek profitable paths to purpose. It also opens up the possibility that there is much to learn from, and understand, outside a business's four walls. Pierrette was aware when business leaders from the developed world came to visit her farm, and she took their interest in her approach as an opportunity to share learnings and experiences. Pierrette has as much to share with business leaders from the other part of the world as with the women in her own community. The lessons are both the same— about hard work, dedication, independence, finding the right partners, and staying true to the mission that drives you.

Pierrette is a business leader. Just like Bill Gates was a business leader at Microsoft. Just like I am a business leader with Connective Impact. Just like my father was a business leader with the local plumbing tool business he ran for 30 years. Just like Meg Whitman was a business leader twice, with eBay and then Hewlett Packard. Business leaders all struggle with the same worries around financial liquidity and success, with confidence and managing teams, with long-term sustainability and relevance. That connectedness, both through real touchpoints or virtual, will only become more unavoidable as businesses recognize the power of collaboration the world over.

LESSONS LEARNED: Corporate social responsibility has evolved as our planet has become more connected, both virtually and through personal touchpoints. Companies that recognize the power of that connectedness, and the opportunity to learn from other leaders outside of their immediate zone of influence, will be stewardship champions, taking social and environmental impact to another level. They will set examples for other leaders to follow and make the real change we need.

CHAPTER SIX

Social Enterprise:
Personal Triumph and
Changing the World

Recently I gave a presentation on private-public-partnerships, something I do quite often. I sat next to a senior vice president from a prominent food company. We were sharing our thoughts on risks, opportunities, and examples of partnerships to address some of the world's most critical challenges, including poverty. I sat next to this man for over an hour, and every point he raised communicated the message that *businesses are built to do good things*.

That's a pretty powerful statement. Businesses are now BUILT to do good?

He isn't the first one to make remarks like this. For the last few days, I have been tracking social media to get a sense of how Fortune 500 leaders refer to social or environmental responsibility. Just in the last week, the number of times I read a quote attributing business success to social impact is more than 50. **FIFTY** times (and I assume I only caught a snippet of what's really out there) major corporate leaders have been quoted **JUST THIS WEEK** opining on the role of business as a force for good. One went so far as to say that there is *no point for business, if not to make the world better.* Whoa. That's a powerful statement, too!

Have we really moved from business being all about profitmaking, to the other extreme, where business exists only to make the world a better place?

Hardly. Even if business moves fast, it doesn't move *that* fast. It seems inconceivable that all corporate leaders really feel this way. And, while I'm sure there is serious selection bias in the social media I follow, we can argue that we have clearly made substantial progress as a global society around the notion of business as the example for social goodness.

It's almost impossible to ignore news headlines, blogs, magazine articles, and entire books (including this one) reviewing the latest trends in business, especially around its role as a social impact leader. For every reason we've outlined in this book, and many more, it's unavoidable for businesses to succeed without considering social and/or environmental impact in some way, shape, or form. Taking it farther, there is a clear movement toward cementing business' role in leading us down the path of social and environmental impact as permanent.

Nothing exhibits this trend more than the evolution of the "B Corp." "B Corps" are companies that define themselves as balancing profit and purpose. My company, Connective Impact, is a B Corp, and for that I am immensely proud. I wouldn't have it any other way. I have to practice what I continually preach to clients aiming to engage partners around social and environmental impact programs. All companies that receive a "B Corporation" certification go through a vigorous impact assessment process, measuring social and environmental commitments, public transparency, and legal accountability.

Anyone unfamiliar with B Corps may assume that all B Corps are small, niche-based brands, or organizations that work with nonprofits around the Sustainable Development Goals (SDGs), but that is not the case at all. Some of the biggest brands in the world are either already B Corps or are working toward their certification.

In August 2019, *The Economist* profiled the social action of French company, Danone, famous for its yogurt, but becoming better known for another reason: its social impact. While other brands, including Ben and Jerry's, Seventh Generation (both now owned by Unilever), REI, and Patagonia, have been touted for their social activism, environmental responsibility, and engagement on critical issues shaping our planet for many years, when Danone announced its intent to become the first independently owned global conglomerate to seek B Corp Certification, the news made waves.[20]

To think that a multi-billion dollar company, with a presence in 130 countries, could position its impact akin to the other brands currently in the B Corp portfolio was almost preposterous. With its yogurt lines, but also Evian and Volvic waters and Silk-branded plant-based milks, achieving this standard seems far-reaching. It's that challenge that is propelling Danone forward, though, and others are following in its wake.

Emmanuel Faber, Danone's Chief Executive Officer, has been quoted as saying, "We have one planet and one health. Let's commit to protect and nourish both." The company is on target to reach certification by 2030 across all of its branded products.

_____

20. https://www.economist.com/business/2018/08/09/danone-rethinks-the-idea-of-the-firm

Certified

Corporation

From the B Corporation Website:

The B Corp community works toward reduced inequality, lower levels of poverty, a healthier environment, stronger communities, and the creation of more high-quality jobs with dignity and purpose. By harnessing the power of business, B Corps use profits and growth as a means to a greater end: positive impact for their employees, communities, and the environment.

B Corps form a community of leaders and drive a global movement of people using business as a force for good. The values and aspirations of the B Corp community are embedded in the ***B Corp Declaration of Interdependence.***

The B Corp Declaration of Interdependence

We envision a global economy that uses business as a force for good.

This economy is comprised of a new type of corporation—the B Corporation—which is purpose-driven and creates benefit for all stakeholders, not just shareholders.

As B Corporations and leaders of this emerging economy, we believe:

- That we must be the change we seek in the world.

- That all business ought to be conducted as if people and place mattered.

- That, through their products, practices, and profits, businesses should aspire to do no harm and benefit all.

- To do so requires that we act with the understanding that we are dependent upon another and thus responsible for each other and future generations.

B Corp is not the only sustainability certification moving companies to action. There are hundreds in fact. Some you may have heard of (Fair Trade, Organic, Energy Star, LEED, Forest Stewardship Council, 1% for the Planet, Certified Humane), and others you may not have (BioPreferred, EDGE, Fair Labor, the list goes on). The trend toward businesses designing their practices and decision-making around creating a real impact is growing fast, evidenced by the growing body of sustainability labels. Today's workers want to work for companies that say and also *do* the right thing. Employers recognize that there is a whole other world to consider when taking into account how to act, speak, invest, innovate, and change. A massive crop of new businesses is springing up every day responding to this trend.

Introducing the social enterprise.

The term "social enterprise" is part of our business nomenclature nowadays, but certainly wasn't a decade ago. According to the Social Enterprise Alliance (SEA), a trade association of sorts for all U.S.-based social enterprises, what a social enterprise is or isn't can be hard to define, due to the fast evolution of the sector over the last few years. Generally, it "blurs the lines of the traditional business, government, and non-profit sectors."[21] SEA goes on to define a social enterprise as, "Organizations that address a basic unmet need

---

21. https://socialenterprise.us/about/social-enterprise/

or solve a social or environmental problem through a market-driven approach."

According to my friend Russ Stoddard, author of *Rise Up: How to Build a Socially Conscious Business*, a social enterprise "deliberately weaves purpose, social impact, and public benefit into its business model."[22] Russ uses the definition of: a "for profit company that intentionally provides products, services, or business models that benefit society and/or the environment using commercial market strategies." In laymen terms, a social enterprise is a company making money and doing good...at the same time. In which case almost every company nowadays is one, though many don't see themselves that way. And there is still quite a ways to go for many companies in truly transitioning their bureaucracies and processes completely over to full-on sustainability.

Shannon Keith made the transition from pharmaceutical saleswoman to social entrepreneur without knowing the term existed. Her business, Sudara, has made it possible to make money while contributing to a powerful cause. Without intending to, Shannon

22. Stoddard, Russ. "Rise Up: How to Build a Socially Conscious Business Model," 2018: p. 10.

has fulfilled a personal mission to positively affect the world through being a business owner.

Photo courtesy of Shannon Keith

Shannon was born in Riverside, California, to teenage parents who were high school sweethearts. Unable to handle the immense responsibility of raising a child, Shannon's father fell into bad times, joining gangs, battling drug addiction, and engaging in illegal behavior that sent him to prison for most of Shannon's childhood. Shannon's parents divorced, her mom remarried, and Shannon grew up in a big, extended, supportive family, led by her mother who valued kindness, hard work, and loved her deeply.

Likely to counteract the shame she felt over her birth father's behavior, Shannon, an only child, dove relentlessly into her studies. She was motivated to excel. A successful businesswoman by the time she was in her twenties, Shannon traveled to India in 2005 with her husband to dedicate a fresh water well in honor of a family member. The village they visited happened to be a red-light brothel district. The trip changed her life completely, sending her on a new, unpredictable life journey.

While visiting in this red-light district, Shannon came upon a squalor among the female sex workers she could never have even imagined, even with the worst description. Smells from open sewers, shoeless children running around without guardians when they should have been in school, and women of all ages standing around in variations of dress. The experience in Shannon's words was "overwhelming."

Like many might do, Shannon could have shaken her head in disbelief and walked away, never to return, hoping to forget the images she saw that day.

Whether it was divine intervention or something else inexplicable, Shannon stayed—and dug in. Instead of turning her back to the women in the district, Shannon looked inward and considered what solutions she could bring to these women and children.

Shannon noticed the saris. The beautiful, colorful, magical saris. She wondered if she could bring the fabric back to the U.S. and sell it, perhaps making some money for these women, while also bringing them a bit of self-righteousness and independence.

Shannon returned to California, where she lived at the time, and started a non-profit, because, according to Shannon, that's what people did before we knew about social entrepreneurism. Back in 2005, if you wanted to make a difference and help people, a nonprofit was the way to go. The nonprofit produced pajamas from the local fabric of the village she visited, and by selling them, Shannon made money she could send back to the village women in exchange for their labor.

When the TOMS shoe company started in 2006, (TOMS is known for starting the one-for-one model: you buy a pair of shoes, and the company gives a pair to a person in need in another part of the world, similar to This Bar Saves Lives mentioned earlier), Shannon realized that if she built a business to help the women in India, there was something longer lasting, more impactful, and mission fulfilling she could create from her nonprofit.

In 2015, Shannon launched Sudara, an apparel company selling loungeware, pajamas, and other clothing items produced exclusively in India, by former female sex slaves. The women workers are paid fair wages, and thus have the ability to provide for their families—and escape the streets.

Now with a certified B Corp, Shannon hopes to extend her brand into other countries outside of India by scaling and growing her business. In India, Sudara partners with nonprofits to connect with the women at risk. Shannon says it's the hard work and bravery of these nonprofits that are ensuring maximum impact through the collaboration with Sudara. The sex trafficking problem is severe. However, knowing that Sudara and its partners are impacting 200 women and their 300 children in a positive way, has been more fulfilling than Shannon could have ever dreamed of. These women have a livelihood and a future, thanks to Sudara and its partners.

Shannon has put the mission of Sudara front and center. Mission drives the company, not profits, but the company continues to grow and make money even when the mission takes priority. That said, there is no financial safety net. Marketing is expensive and competitive. No matter the size, businesses always grapple with the challenge of making money and remaining profitable when there are so many directions the company is pulled. Shannon believes that profits are still critical, since they keep the lights on, and for Sudara, the women in India in a lifestyle that affords them freedom.

But Shannon also believes that businesses can continue to make money by doing the right thing, particularly within supply chains, and through ethical and fair labor practices. Her sights are set on a profitable future for Sudara, and where Sudara can be a "shining example of empowerment and equity."

As social enterprises become more successful (the Social Enterprise Alliance has over 1,000 member companies alone), the concept behind social entrepreneurship is becoming more attractive to mainstream brands. The questions I've received from several Fortune 500 companies about how social enterprises are paving the way on innovation, or brand marketing, or impact (yes!), or consumer retention have amplified significantly over the last five years. In fact, some of the projects my company is working on now involve partnerships between social enterprises and some of the bigger, more mainstream brands, helping clunkier companies learn how to be more creative and nimble in achieving and measuring impact.

Inc. Magazine recently profiled an example of this type of partnership. In 2016, General Mills purchased start-up and social enterprise EPIC Provisions, a meat-based snack company, known for processing its products in a way that is safe for the environment, and humane to animals. Additionally, the company aims to help test regenerative grazing processes and raise bison, chickens, turkeys, ducks, geese, and bees in a natural environment.[23] According to the article, one of the attractive features of the new snack company to stalwart General Mills was access to millennial customers.

Despite some bumps in the road and the understandable growth pains (EPIC staying true to its original mission and General Mills adapting to some of EPIC's practices in suit), EPIC has grown its revenues four times over, and is helping General Mills innovate and learn at the same time.

In order to find the right social enterprise, innovation partners, or idea generation, some companies have launched their own accelerator programs, or funds, hoping to tap into social entrepreneurial minds to engage on social and environmental issues in a more formidable way.

_____

23. https://www.inc.com/magazine/201811/tom-foster/epic-provisions-general-mills-meat-snacks.html

Here are just a few examples:

- Chobani, the yogurt company started by Turkish immigrant Hamdi Ulukaya, is investing in startup social enterprises to help bring food to more people around the world.

- Unilever started *Unilever Foundry*, a program that invests in startup businesses solving some of the world's growing social challenges, and helping Unilever's business unite around these issues at the same time.

- A number of apparel companies, including Adidas, C&A, PVH, Kering, and Target founded Fashion for Good, an accelerator for innovative companies "with the potential to disrupt the current apparel and textile value chain, bringing a positive environmental and/or social impact."

- Kellogg launched a venture capital fund to invest in food startups testing new foods, ingredients, and packaging to identify new and innovative solutions for its own business.

- Target has launched a program to support startups run by social entrepreneurs testing new approaches that make sales, retail, and customer engagement "better for the planet."

Companies recognize that to evolve and stay relevant, and to make an impact in a long-term, sustainable way, they must consider different types of models, like social enterprises or B Corps, as viable and necessary partners.

Businesses have begun to engage with a variety of social and environmental partners in a way that brings resources to diverse programs when direct engagement by the business may not be feasible. Connective Impact, for example, is a contributing member of 1% for the Planet. Every year we, along with hundreds of other companies, give 1 percent of our gross revenues to organizations that are making improvements for our planet. Examples include local and global environmental organizations, nature preservation programs, and alliances that bring together different interests to address critical issues like ocean health or climate change. Giving like this is something we would do anyway, because we believe in the power of collective action toward social, environmental, and economic change. But to know there is an organization to make that commitment easier goes to show how far we've come as corporate citizens. Organizations like 1% allow companies to be philanthropic. They also help those who are socially and environmentally minded to overcome the challenges of embedding philanthropic practices into their businesses.

LESSONS LEARNED: The notion of purpose is evolving as new ways of doing business take into account the personal and professional impact of doing the right thing. Companies, and their leaders, want to invest in decision-making and innovative pograms that have a long-term positive impact on the world around us. Newer business models, like the B Corp, make this possible.

CHAPTER SEVEN

Shifting Winds: Lasting Leadership and a Better Planet

Last year I was in Nairobi, Kenya for a convening of big brands and social enterprises. We were meeting to discuss better ways to collaborate. I was asked to facilitate a session with the big brands on partnership for social impact, and, as I sometimes do in these scenarios, I led the 50 or so attendees in a "four corners" exercise where participants self-select which corner of the room to stand in based on their response to a particular question.

The question was: "What is the main role business should play in society?"

The answers were: (1) produce goods for consumption; (2) advocate for pro-business government policies; (3) inspire change in local communities; (4) invest in innovation.

This is a tough question for business execs to answer, especially those who work on social and environmental impact strategies for their companies. The conundrum of which answer to pick was intentional. The exercise encouraged the brand reps to truly think about what their role should be, even though many may believe their role is all of the above.

Which answer do you think everyone picked?

Of the 50 or so participants in the room, 49 traveled to the corner assigned to "produce goods for consumption."

I asked several of the corporate execs participating to explain their answer. Generally, the rationale centered around the framing of the question: When you ask a company about its "main" role, it cannot deny that its main function is to produce goods (or services, in some cases). That is why a business is a business (and not a charity, or government). When I pressed some of the attendees on the portion of the question that reads: "should play in society," most agreed that at their core, businesses exist to provide a good or service in exchange for money. That is what makes their entity function.

A few did change their answers after we discussed what a business role in society looks like. That's because while businesses exist to produce goods for consumption, they also exist for all of the other reasons we gave in our exercise. We need businesses to help advocate for critical issues with lawmakers and decision makers. Businesses are inherently leaders on innovation, and they also most certainly are needed to inspire social change. There cannot be any denying, however, that businesses do exist to make money, and that has been, and will always be, their priority. That doesn't take away any rationale, however, for businesses to also be intent on doing the right thing. What it means, though, is that businesses need a clear sense of the return on their investments in issues that pertain to social and environmental impact. There must be a clear business case, the costs must be in line with expectations, and the benefit must be positive for cash flow.

This may seem lofty, but it's happening. The growth of social enterprise models is just one example of the recognition that making money and "doing good" are not mutually exclusive.

One example I often share with clients is that of McDonalds, who despite some challenges in always doing the "right thing," has figured out ways to continually make money as they change their methods of doing business to improve our planet. For example, the company replaced its styrofoam clamshell packaging containers in 1990 with help from the Environmental Defense Fund and saved an estimated $6 million in doing so. The new packaging also eliminated 300 million pounds of packaging from its waste stream.[24] It's pretty remarkable that this action was initiated nearly 30 years ago when CSR and sustainability were hardly known in the world of brand investment.

Say what you will about the company, and whether you like their food or not, their work to address carbon emissions from cattle, change sourcing practices toward grass-fed beef and local produce, investing in youth education opportunities worldwide, and partnering with social impact players, like the Rainforest Alliance and TechnoServe, to address the SDGs is not something to sweep under the rug.[25] The company is taking seriously its role as a brand leader to make positive change, and the return on their investment? McDonalds' stock price has more than doubled in the last five years despite stagnant sales. The company has found ways to cut costs by using more responsible practices and planning for a more sustainable future.

---

24. https://www.edf.org/partnerships/mcdonalds

25. https://corporate.mcdonalds.com/corpmcd/scale-for-good/using-our-scale-for-good/un-sustainable-development-goals.html

According to a study commissioned jointly by Camp-bell Soup Company and Verizon, aptly named "Project ROI," being socially and environmentally responsible has a positive impact on sales and employee produc-tivity. Additionally, the report found that over a 15-year period, companies with effective CSR programs have on average increased shareholder value by $1.28 billion.[26] The report looked at causality, so the conclu-sion can be made that investments in "doing the right thing" can positively impact the bottom line.

Unfortunately, though, that isn't always the case. I've spoken to many companies that had to stop certain CSR programs because the company was losing money due entirely to that investment.

It must be true that companies have found the sweet spot, though, between making money and making positive social and environmental investments that also improve communities, and our planet. Otherwise there wouldn't be headline after headline announcing new partnerships and corporate-led efforts to address SDG-type challenges. As worlds around us collide through accessibility, it's also impossible to ignore

---

26. https://projectroi.com/

the alternative of NOT doing the right thing by stake-holders.

One interesting campaign I read about last week, initi-ated by Oxfam America, claims Whole Foods, a gener-ally responsible and forward learning brand around social and environmental impact issues, is ignoring inhumane and dangerous working conditions in its supply chains, especially for women, and particularly in seafood. The attack is part of the nonprofit's "Behind the Barcodes" reporting that looked at poor labor conditions among retailers' supply chains. Walmart and Albertsons had the highest responsibility scores. Whole Foods and Kroger, the lowest.[27]

Campaigns like these have the tendency to call out companies that need a push to make changes, even if they are already doing a lot to fix problems or be outwardly responsible. The opportunities to create positive change are really endless. The challenge is prioritizing the most necessary actions, being mindful of stakeholders and their needs, being honest about shortcomings, and finding ways to maintain profitability while still doing the right thing. Every. Single. Time. It's not always easy. But it's possible. And necessary.

---

27. https://www.oxfamamerica.org/take-action/campaign/food-farming-and-hunger/behind-the-barcodes/

In a 2015 study,[28] Nielsen asked 30,000 consumers in 60 countries about what influences their buying behavior. The survey found that two-thirds of respondents would be willing to pay a higher price for more sustainable products. Believing in the brands' willingness to do the right thing played an important role in consumers' responses. This goes to show that doing the right thing matters to a brand's image, and to its bottom line. It takes some pretty significant consumer shifts to allow that message to set in sometimes, though.

When Larry Fink, the CEO of BlackRock, one of the largest institutional investment managers in the world, sent a public letter to "CEOs everywhere" titled "Sense of Purpose" at the start of 2018, it was a pretty obvious signal that times had fully changed. Calling for more purpose in corporate decision making, and a shifting mindset toward responsibility, Fink's letter made waves and started us down the road toward purposeful corporate investing and decision making in as stark a way as conceivable. This is our future.

Fink writes:

28. https://www.nielsen.com/us/en/press-room/2015/consumer-goods-brands-that-demonstrate-commitment-to-sustainability-outperform.html

Larry Fink's Letter to CEOs Everywhere

As BlackRock approaches its 30th anniversary this year, I have had the opportunity to reflect on the most pressing issues facing investors today and how BlackRock must adapt to serve our clients more effectively.

The public expectations of your company have never been greater. Society is demanding that companies, both public and private, serve a social purpose. To prosper over time, every company must not only deliver financial performance, but also show how it makes a positive contribution to society. Companies must benefit all of their stakeholders, including shareholders, employees, customers, and the communities in which they operate.

Without a sense of purpose, no company, either public or private, can achieve its full potential. It will ultimately lose the license to operate from key stakeholders. It will succumb to short-term pressures to distribute earnings, and, in the process, sacrifice investments in employee development, innovation, and capital expenditures that are necessary for long-term growth. It will remain exposed to activist campaigns that articulate a clearer goal, even if that goal serves only the shortest and narrowest of objectives. And, ultimately, that company will provide subpar returns to the investors who depend on it to finance their retirement, home purchases, or higher education.

The statement of long-term strategy is essential to understanding a company's actions and policies, its preparation for potential challenges, and the context of its shorter-term decisions. Your company's strategy must articulate a path to achieve financial performance. To sustain that performance, however, you must also understand the societal impact of your business as well as the ways that broad, structural trends—from slow wage growth to rising automation to climate change—affect your potential for growth.

Companies must ask themselves: What role do we play in the community? How are we managing our impact on the environment? Are we working to create a diverse workforce? Are we adapting to technological change? Are we providing the retraining and opportunities that our employees and our business will need to adjust to an increasingly automated world? Are we using behavioral finance and other tools to prepare workers for retirement, so that they invest in a way that will help them achieve their goals?

Today, our clients—who are your company's owners—are asking you to demonstrate the leadership and clarity that will drive not only their own investment returns, but also the prosperity and security of their fellow citizens. We look forward to engaging with you on these issues.

LESSONS LEARNED: Businesses are always examining their role in society, and being leaders around social, environmental, and economic impact presents no exception. Leading companies have figured out how to represent their business interests while, at the same time, making decisions that have humanistic and empathetic outcomes. Stakeholders are responding well to this hybrid, and that will only continue as investors, partners, governments, and indeed consumers support those companies that are doing the right thing, without question, and without hesitation.

Conclusion

Thanks to Arthur Karuletwa, my friend, who I admire and learn from always, for writing this final chapter with me.

True world changers have the ability to transcend their physical presence and almost step into another place, time, or being to listen, learn, and act based on the empathy they feel. As business leaders open themselves up to this transcendent experience, either via travel, virtual reality, reading, or engaging with employees who have different perspectives and backgrounds, the ability to lead with intention will skyrocket. This will cause a permanent shift in how we think of money, success, and wellbeing. As evidenced by the stories in this book, we are on our way there.

What will that next step look like? How will we know when the corporate titans of today are fully transcendent, looking at purpose and profit as mutually exclusive and co-dependent? I look to my friend Arthur Karuletwa for inspiration on this topic on a regular basis.

During a 2011 visit to Seattle to meet with the ethical sourcing team at Starbucks Coffee Company, I met a very tall, unforgettable man named Arthur. Arthur was somewhat new to Starbucks, having joined the Global Coffee team from a consultancy he led during his years in Rwanda. Arthur presented his work on a traceability program, which enabled customers to learn about the origins of their coffee just by scanning a code off the back of the coffee bag. Information about who grows our coffee was (and in many cases still is) hard to come by.

Arthur had amazing stories to share of the coffee farmers behind each batch, and he shared a portion of those stories with us during our meeting. Arthur emphasizes that these stories are not just a matter of putting poetic language around the coffee, but rather, he believes that these stories are, and should be told, through the lens of the supply chain itself. More specifically, Arthur sees each story as a journey, carrying with it the survival instincts that were necessary for the coffee growers to live and thrive and grow the coffee. Going deeper, Arthur truly believes that the journey of each coffee grower is about the preservation of all of us, of humanity.

Arthur was born in Uganda after his parents fled their native home nation of Rwanda in 1975. At the age of two, Arthur and his family then fled to Kenya during the 1977 war where he and his five siblings (four brothers and one sister) spent the next 10 years. By 1987, the pressures on Kenya from the constant influx of Rwandan refugees became overbearing, which led to an eventual exodus back to Uganda soon after the National Resistant Army took power back from the dictator Idi Amin. Arthur and his siblings had never known life other than as a refugee, and again, this move was promised to be temporary, since Arthur's family ultimately wanted to return to their home in Rwanda. While growing up, Arthur and his siblings did their best to immerse themselves in whichever community they lived, despite the scarlet letter that bears the stripes of being in constant refugee status.

As a 6-foot, 6-inch young teen, Arthur spent his free time playing soccer, but soon took up basketball, an easy switch given his height. Arthur quickly fell in love with the game, and the sport loved him back with invitations to several basketball camps sprouting up within the capital city of Kampala in Uganda.

At one of the camps, a basketball coach from Oxnard, California spotted Arthur. After watching him play repeatedly, the coach offered Arthur a scholarship to attend his junior college. This was 1993. Arthur was 18 years old. Just as he felt his life could settle as he sought a future for himself in the United States, and as his family hoped to return to Rwanda, the Rwandan Genocide took over in 1994. Despite promise of nation-wide peace for the Rwandan people, instead they experienced cataclysmic ethnic cleansing. Arthur's entire extended family, and his extended ethnic community in Rwanda, were wiped out in a matter of days.

Arthur's communication with his coach, and with it the opportunity to play basketball, was naturally diminished and subdued. Survival with, and for his countrymen and women, was his family's priority. When the last machete was laid down, it had been 100 days of one of the worst forms of human atrocities in recent history. There were two groups of people: those who died undignified; and those who seemingly rose from the dead, still feeling undignified.

Arthur's coach had transferred to Ventura Junior College, and yet never gave up on him. The two reconnected when the U.S. Embassy re-opened in Rwanda as the nation picked itself back up. Arthur made it to the U.S. after all.

After two years at Ventura College, he transferred to The Master's University, where he played basketball and studied business. Arthur never forgot where he came from; it never left his mind that a million of his fellow countrymen and women had lost their lives over the most valuable human asset—their identity. This thought stayed with him all the years he was in college, while his nation tried to rebuild from the endless skulls and bones, blood stained rivers, and a people haunted by and among themselves.

After college, Arthur found a love/hate relationship with coffee.

Rwanda has a history of coffee growing dating back to the 1930s. The drink was introduced in colonial Rwanda, yet its growers were suppressed during those times, causing an endless cycle of poverty. The feelings of dislike toward that history, and yet love for the product, led Arthur to learn more about the industry. He ended up interning at a green (unroasted) coffee storage facility in Seattle. Soon after that, he took a position at Millstone Coffee, owned by Procter and Gamble. There, Arthur managed the Pacific Northwest sales distribution.

The recognition that more could be done in his home country of Rwanda nagged him, however. He saw how hard the country was struggling to rebuild, even 10 years after the genocide, and believed something had to change.

In 2004, Arthur returned to Rwanda, in part to help rebuild, but also to heal the wounds of pain and inadequacy he felt having survived the genocide, when so many didn't.

Under the Ministry of Agriculture, Arthur led a program to revamp the fledging coffee sector, reporting into the office of the President of Rwanda. Here, under the mentorship of one of the most innovative leaders of our time, Paul Kagame, he learned about the plans to reconcile a nation once divided by the atrocities of a horrific past through its most precious commodity: agriculture.

While in Rwanda, Arthur realized that to make agriculture work for this struggling economy, they needed a way to tell the story of the product, in this case—coffee, from farm to sale. This would help educate about the product and its origins to a world that had in many ways forgotten about the Rwandan people. Arthur needed to create a market system for Rwandan coffee that so far simply didn't exist. According to *CNN Money*, Arthur "...began to modernize the market. He set up programs to teach fertilizing methods and created co-ops of farmers."[29] He found ways to ensure coffee farmers made more money. He revolutionized how the market operated, brought more efficiency, and cut out extra costs.

---

29. https://money.cnn.com/magazines/business2/business2_
    archive/2006/08/01/8382246/

Arthur founded a roaster/retail establishment called Bourbon Coffee in Kigali. The company grew fast and propelled growth in local consumption of Rwanda coffee. Eventually eight stores operated across three continents. Arthur had become the lynchpin behind Rwandan coffee's success. He truly represented the country's bright future.

In 2006, Arthur joined President Kagame and Starbucks CEO at the time, Howard Schultz, in Seattle, to celebrate Starbucks' first Rwandan coffee. Arthur was seen as an important connection for the U.S. coffee market to the land of one thousand hills.

With a few more coffee buying and marketing roles under his belt, Arthur eventually became an adviser to Starbucks, taking on a role of East African Adviser and Strategist. It was during this time that I met Arthur in Seattle. Within two years, Arthur was leading traceability in 23 countries for coffee, cocoa, and tea for the global coffee behemoth. When Arthur speaks, people listen.

Arthur's journey is symbolic of power in two ways. On one hand, when greed and power take over, we can experience horrible things, like during the Rwandan Genocide. When brilliance has power, on the other hand, creativity can be heard, and voices make change, as in the case when Arthur rebuilt the coffee sector in his home country. His ability to make an impact at one of the most powerful companies in the world, and with one of the most pivotal political figures in modern day history, shows that some of the most hidden stories can change the world. It also shows us that change from within is possible. Leadership for impact is feasible within even the biggest companies.

After traveling back to Rwanda, Arthur often posts on his Facebook and Instagram pages his inspiring stories, full of words of wisdom and teachings.

He recently posted this, and I asked if I could include it in this book. He agreed. I cannot think of a better message to carry forward as businesses work to change the trajectory of their past toward a more profitable, successful, and purposeful future.

Photo courtesy of Arthur Karuletwa

Chronicles of a Place: "True sustainability is like experiencing the holistic convergence of a product, its habitat, and its producer. It's the forging of an economy for all three.

And because of this, sustainability is ultimately an ethical issue. There is no economic reason to do anything for some person or for some future generation, other than it's the right thing to do. I have come to realize that we owe a debt to those of the past who created the opportunities we have today. And we can only repay that debt to those of the future. And with every payment of that debt, our lives become better. And because of this, we fulfill our purpose for being here. That is why I will always come back here." – *Arthur*

Lessons Learned

1. Being truthful about misgivings, shortcomings, or opportunities to improve is always preferred over lack of transparency. Dedicated leadership and employees, particularly those who believe in the corporate mission, can help a company stay on track with its social impact. Contrary to what we believed in the '80s, greed is never good. Understanding global contexts will help businesses make informed and proper decisions for long-term sustainability in regions where customers, employees, suppliers, and other stakeholders are most meaningful.

2. For decades, companies were seen as conglomerates simply out to make money and provide products for consumption. While some of those aims have not changed, the role of business leaders within companies is evolving, and the role of empathy and an interest in improving our planet is shifting the mission of many companies into beacons of social and environmental change. This evolution takes many shapes and sizes, but even the companies with the most challenging history can make progress and affect positive change.

3. When companies recognize that there are other needs outside of the philanthropic domain for their active engagement, and they take ownership of their role to steer the ship in a direction of positive change, making the world a better place is not only possible, it's inevitable.

4. Gaining awareness and exposure to the world around us is what makes us the most effective at changing the world, and passing that value on within our four walls will drive the agenda farther. Empathy is a critical skill in business to ensure change is coming from a place of true meaning and consideration of needs outside one's own perspective.

5. Corporate social responsibility has evolved as our planet has become more connected, both virtually and through personal touchpoints. Companies that recognize the power of that connectedness, and the opportunity to learn from other leaders outside of their immediate zone of influence, will be stewardship champions, taking social and environmental impact to another level. They will set examples for other leaders to follow and make the real change we need.

7. The notion of purpose is evolving as new ways of doing business take into account the personal and professional impact of doing the right thing. Companies, and their leaders, want to invest in decision-making and innovative programs that have a long-term positive impact on the world around us. Newer business models, like the B Corp, make this possible.

8. Businesses are always examining their role in society, and being leaders around social, environmental, and economic impact presents no exception. Leading companies have figured out how to represent their business interests while at the same time, making decisions that have humanistic and empathetic outcomes. Stakeholders are responding well to this hybrid, and that will only continue as investors, partners, governments, and indeed consumers support those companies that are doing the right thing, without question, and without hesitation.

Acknowledgments

Exactly two weeks before the release of my first book, *ChangeSeekers: Finding Your Path to Impact,* I learned that the publisher I had been working with for more than a year, had shut its doors without telling a soul. The staff had been let go with no warning, and the authors (including me) were heading down a pretty fast creek without a paddle. There were many legal and financial issues to deal with, but my number one priority was saving my book from falling into a black hole, something that would have devastated me after putting so much work into it. With the help of some amazing people, including my author colleagues, Russ Stoddard, Tony Bridwell, David Savage, Dee Ann Turner, Mike Thompson, Jeremy Sparks, Darryl Womack, Mark Colgate, Mike Schindler, Dan Pontefract, and Kyle McNeal, plus former publishing house staff Bobby Kuber, Anna McHargue, Jim Mhoon, Jana Good, Rae Felte, and Todd Carman, I was able to save the book's life and ensure its publication. Maggie Powell did the heavy lifting. She was my saving grace.

That experience taught me a lot about the realities of publishing, but what's more, that trust and integrity can be broken. As someone who believes in peoples' goodness and kindness, above much else, this was a life lesson I'll never get over. As someone who is also pretty glass-half-full, however, I was able to make some amazing lemonade out of lemons, first by learning so much from the aforementioned author colleagues, but also in setting the stage for this book. I wasn't sure after writing a first book whether I'd want to write a second book. After having to re-compose *ChangeSeekers* in just two weeks, it became obvious that a second book was not only doable, it would be necessary. I knew that I needed the control of a full process, not just a piece of one.

In writing *Purposeful Profits*, I have to thank my author colleagues for inspiring me by their own writing, and intense passion to get their words out for those to read and learn from. I owe my editor, Anna McHargue, more thanks than there are words on endless pages of paper. Anna, who edited *ChangeSeekers* with me as well, has become a true, lasting friend, and the ability to work with her is just seamless. She's a kind-hearted, open, and sweet soul, who just makes you want to do and be better. Her book, *People Are Good* is a must read for anyone who wants a little pick me up on a bad day.

Despite all the dirt hurled our way sometimes, People are Good! I have learned that and more from Anna.

Thanks to John Mata and David Carroll for their beautiful design support, Maggie Powell, for helping me get this book ready and readable, and Marissa Rosen for helping me get the message behind this book out to the masses.

I am beyond grateful to Tawiah, Pierrette, Shayne, Marcy, Erin, Shannon, and Arthur for letting me profile them in the book, and Julie Curtis and Clinton Lee helping me translate and coordinate with Pierrette. Thanks to Lisa Curtis for your connection to Pierrette, and for setting the bar so high for other entrepreneurs by making such an amazing difference in this world. Thanks to Beatrice Moulianitaki, Hazel Culley, and Bob Bailey for connecting me to your friends and colleagues, both to profile in this book and for research. Thanks to Todd O'Rourke for your important contributions as well.

I owe a tremendous amount of gratitude to the clients of Connective Impact, who I have the absolute fortune of working with every day. Each of you inspires me to work harder and faster to find the right partners to keep your goals in line as you change the world.

To all of my friends and family, who always support me and who are my cheerleaders, thank you for keeping me grounded and humble, and yet recognizing that the work I do is important and needed.

For my husband, who listens to me babble about crazy ideas all the time. Thank you for always making me feel like my ideas have merit, and that my work is meaningful and needed. And, thank you for inspiring me with the work you do every day making the world safer and fairer for our Veterans, who are so underserved.

Finally, to my boys. You are the reasons I work so hard to make this world better. I know that the future is bright with you in it, and I have every ounce of confidence that you will take your legacy seriously to work hard, be kind, and always root for the Cleveland Browns no matter how bad they are.

About the Author

Joanne Sonenshine is Founder + CEO of Connective Impact, an advisory firm aiding organizations in partnership strategy and fundraising diversification to address social, environmental, and economic development challenges through collaboration.

A trained development economist, Joanne has devoted her career to helping decision-makers, corporate leaders, and entrepreneurs coalesce to create more formidable impact in their work.

Joanne's first book, *ChangeSeekers: Finding Your Path to Impact*, documents how to overcome fear, uncertainty, and risk aversion to seek fulfillment in one's life, and truly make a difference.

Joanne lives in Arlington, Virginia, with her husband and two boys.

Humanitarian/Origin Trip Travel Resources

Raptim
www.raptim.org

Omaze
www.omaze.com

Operation Groundswell
www.operationgroundswell.com

UBELONG
www.ubelong.org

CHOICE Humanitarian
www.choicehumanitarian.org

Cross-Cultural Solutions
www.crossculturalsolutions.org

CONNECTIVE IMPACT

WE MAKE LASTING PROGRESS	ACHIEVE THE RIGHT GOALS	OUR RESULTS ARE PROVEN
At Connective Impact, we work to keep commitments on track and bring like-minded organizations together to make progress effective and lasting.	Our six step approach helps clients achieve the right goals for their organization. Learn more about our process and download sample templates we use with our clients.	Our clients are global noprofits, corporations, governments and social entrepreneurs seeking a healthier, safer and more productive planet by working collectively.

Learn about Connective Impact,
your partnerships and collaboration advisors
by visiting: **www.connectiveimpact.com**

Connective Impact is proud to be co-founder of
MagCollective.com

MAG
COLLECTIVE

CPSIA information can be obtained
at www.ICGtesting.com
Printed in the USA
FFHW011903080419
51588094-57028FF